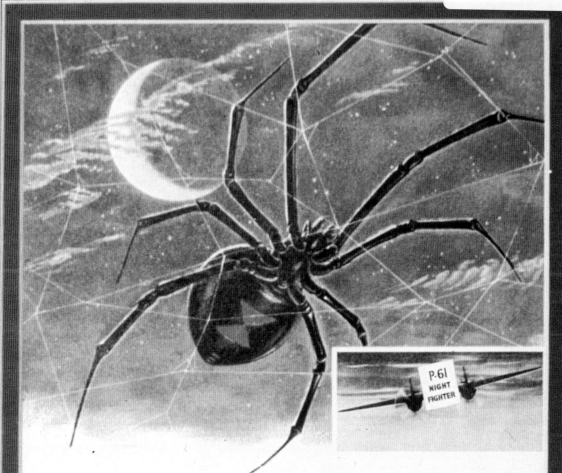

BLACK WIDOW is
the name and the general idea

The Black Widow spider is a formidable creature. It lurks in the dark . . . attacks unseen . . . cuts down its prey with poison 15 times stronger than rattlesnake venom

THE NAME "Black Widow" is a natural for the Army's new warplane, the P-61 *night fighter*.

The "Black Widow" airplane is the first designed-for-the-purpose night fighter. Its job is to attack the enemy by night. To protect air-strips and beachheads . . . to guard cities . . . to cover unloading operations. To intrude behind enemy lines and harass trains and airfields, destroy *matériel*.

The Northrop "Black Widow" is the largest, most powerful pursuit plane ever built. It has unusual speed. It can also loaf, almost hover as it hides in the night sky. Its firepower is devastating. It can take off swiftly and land slowly in the dark.

In cooperation with the Army Air Forces, the Northrop group designed the "Black Widow". You'll hear more from it . . . the deadly P-61.

NORTHROP AIRCRAFT, INC.
NORTHROP FIELD, HAWTHORNE, CALIFORNIA
MEMBER AIRCRAFT WAR PRODUCTION COUNCIL, INC.

NORTHROP
Designers and Builders of the
P-61 *'Black Widow'* NIGHT FIGHTER

Northrop P-61
BLACK WIDOW

The Complete History and Combat Record

Garry R. Pape with John M. and Donna Campbell

Motorbooks International
Publishers & Wholesalers ®

To those visionaries who brought the Black Widow to life, and the intrepid crews who flew it in war and peace.

First published in 1991 by Motorbooks International Publishers & Wholesalers, P O Box 2, 729 Prospect Avenue, Osceola, WI 54020 USA

Motorbooks International books are also available at discounts in bulk quantity for industrial or sales-promotional use. For details write to Special Sales Manager at the Publisher's address

Library of Congress Cataloging-in-Publication Data
Pape, Garry R.
    Northrop P-61 Black Widow / Garry R. Pape, John M. Campbell, Donna Campbell.
        p.   cm.
    ISBN 0-87938-509-X
    1. Black Widow (Fighter planes)   I. Campbell, John M. II. Campbell, Donna.   III. Title.
UG1242.F5P36 1991
358.4'3—dc20   90-24611

Printed and bound in Hong Kong

On the front cover: A technician checks the front landing gear on a P-61B. *Northrop*

On the back cover: The Black Widow spat death from four .50 caliber machine guns in the dorsal turret and four 20 mm cannon in the belly. *Wolford*

On the frontispiece: A wartime Northrop advertisement touts the Black Widow's abilities. *Northrop*

On the title page: Engine heaters were necessary in the -35 degree Fahrenheit cold at Ladd Field, Alaska in February 1944. *USAF*

Contents

Foreword

I was one of the twenty pilots the Army Air Forces assigned to start the night fighter program. This book details these events extremely well. For those of us who lived the operational aspects, this book is a nostalgic adventure. For aviation history, this is a very valuable contribution. For others with an interest in World War II aviation and the early days of electronics in aviation, it is most interesting and essential to the understanding of much of the pressures and needs in the "early days."

I am, of course, prejudiced, for from my first flight in a P-61 on September 4, 1944, it was love at first flight. I had modest success flying the Widow, but

Maj. Carroll "Snuffy" Smith, the highest scoring USAAF night fighter of WW II, in the cockpit of a P-61 after his return to the States at Van Nuys Army Air Base, California.

more importantly, I had more confidence in this aircraft than any of the other fifty-seven types of aircraft I flew spanning thirty years from the PT-13 biplane to the Mach 2 F-106.

Northrop P-61 Black Widow covers our frustrations in the early days of World War II at our inability to do the night air defense job and our casting about for better weapons. The P-61, when it arrived, gave us a weapon system far superior in all respects to what we were using against the Japanese. The Mosquito used in Europe was better than the P-70 we had, but the P-61 improved their capability as well. The P-61, being on the leading edge of technology, received mixed reaction from military leaders, but it was able to prove itself even to the most skeptical. The quality of our training early on was very poor. For example, the first aerial target I shot at was a Japanese aircraft. The training improved rapidly as the war progressed; however, our success with the P-61 was due in large measure to its admirable flying characteristics. She was a very forgiving airplane, and many of us probably owe our lives to the advanced design thinking by Jack Northrop and his crew.

When I returned from the Pacific in 1945, Jack Northrop invited me to his office for coffee and discussion. He asked for comments and criticism of the P-61. My only criticism was the pilot's canopy latch. After all the time I had spent flying the P-61, that was my most serious complaint. That sure speaks well for the overall design and performance. Any combat aircraft you can completely stall at 200 or 300 feet and recover without crashing is something special. As stated

earlier, my first flight in a P-61 was on September 4, 1944, at Eagle Farm Depot in Brisbane, Australia. The aircraft were being assembled there after sea shipment from the United States. I shot down my first aircraft with a P-61 on October 7, 1944. We were self-taught, so the ease of transition is obvious.

The use of the P-61 was hampered by the old Army concept of anti-aircraft guns for defense; more than one area had this disadvantage. All too often the night fighters were hampered by Army anti-aircraft commanders, in charge of air defense, who prevented them from taking off to challenge an incoming raid. We had to prove ourselves over and over to be taken seriously and allowed to do our job as best we could.

The P-61's looks were very deceiving. It looked awkward and ungainly for a fighter. This aided some of the wagers with our day fighter friends, many of whom were made poorer due to their hasty bets on performance ability. I profited from this experience. However, if I could have flown the Widow like John Myers [Northrop test pilot], I would have done even better.

The P-61 progressed from skepticism to acceptance for its many uses. Much innovation was brought about due to its adaptability. It led the way to the current crop of great all-weather aircraft. It was a pleasure to have known the Widow, and I am delighted that Garry Pape with John and Donna Campbell have recorded this very valuable part of aviation history in such a comprehensive and easy reading style. Every aviation enthusiast must have this book.
Col. Carroll C. Smith
USAF (Retired)

Acknowledgments

Many people have assisted me in putting the Black Widow story together over the past twenty-six years. In the next few pages, I have listed all those who have been so patient with me during prolonged interviews, provided volumes of correspondence and copies of documents, and took the time to tape remembrances.

There are a number of professional historians who have been instrumental in making this project possible. My sincere gratitude goes to the late naval historians William M. and James H. Belote. When I was a teenager, these gentlemen spent much time at my home while Bill Belote was dating my sister (eventually he married her). It was at this time that they introduced me to aviation history—taking me to the University of California at Berkeley libraries, to airports, and providing a plethora of aviation magazines. Historian Kenn C. Rust, as editor at the American Aviation Historical Society, gave me great encouragement and assistance in early 1966, when I was beginning my research into this little known and documented aircraft.

My heartfelt thanks goes to the late Brig. Gen. Winston W. "Winkie" Kratz who allowed me to make a number of visits to his home to pick his brain, and answered a barrage of questions over many years. He was quite kind in providing needed guidance and appreciated advice. Thanks also to Col. William C. Odell who provided similar assistance over the years.

USAF retired Lt. Col. William H. Greenhalgh contributed research from the US Air Force Historical Research Center at Maxwell Air Force Base in Alabama. A number of Northrop people have also contributed substantially to this project. Hugo R. Pink provided both information and assistance in contacting past and present Northrop employees who had been associated with the Widow. Roy Wolford has graciously provided many beautiful color transparencies. Northrop historian Dr. Ira E. Chart kindly opened all of his files for my use and did extensive research in my behalf. Fellow historical enthusiasts Gerald H. Balzer and Warren E. Thompson also made their vast collections available to me. To all I am deeply indebted.

Finally, I owe much to my wife, Barbara J. Pape, for her constant encouragement, running of errands, typing and putting up with the lot of an aviation widow during the research and writing of the manuscript.

Garry R. Pape
Rowland Heights, California
September 1990

We would like to acknowledge the support and invaluable assistance provided by the following: Jack Moses, Stu Ostler, James Crowder, Ph.D., Don Klinko, Lura M. Casey, Connie Robinson, James H. Kitchens III, Ph.D. and to all those who have so kindly provided photographs, negatives, slides and transparencies. We have strived to give complete and accurate credit with each picture in this book. Once again Jeffrey L. Ethell has provided us both material and very valuable guidance during this project. I would also like to take this opportunity to express my thanks to Ruth and F. D. Campbell for their continuing encouragement and support during this effort.

John M. Campbell
Donna Campbell
Oklahoma City, Oklahoma
September 1990

Assistance has also been rendered by the following:

Aircraft development
Irving L. Ashkenas (engineering)
Fred J. Baum (P-61 project engineer)
Vic Bertagna (engineering)
Walter J. Cerny (assistant chief engineer)
Willard R. Clay (project engineer)
Herbert DeCenzo (chief of aerodynamics)
John Hathaway (manufacturing)
M. Scott Johnson (technical representative, Pacific)
John W. Myers (chief test pilot and vice president)
John K. Northrop (president and chief of design)
Vladimir H. Pavlecka (chief of research)
Hugo R. Pink (test operations)
G. H. Pope (aerodynamics)
Maj. Gen. Marshall S. Roth, USAF (Ret) (AAF project engineer)
Albert M. Schwartz (design coordinator)
Dr. William R. Sears (chief of aerodynamics)
Max R. Stanley (test pilot)
Sterling C. Walter (manufacturing and modification departments)
S. E. Weaver (stress group)

John M. Wild (project engineer)
Roy Wolford (photo department)

Aircraft usage
Julius E. Alford (6th NFS)
Alvin E. Anderson (425th NFS)
Lt. Col. Roy M. Atwell, USAF (Ret) (416th NFS)
Paul H. Baldwin (547th NFS)
Mack Ballard (421st NFS)
Lt. Col. Frank L. Bosch (547th NFS)
William T. Bradley (421st NFS)
Lt. Col. Jack F. Bradner, USAF (Ret) (6th NFS)
George C. Brainard (NF Training)
Robert N. Buck (TWA—Project Thunderstorm)
Allen S. Clark (415th NFS)
Col. Robert D. Curtis, USAF (Ret) (548th NFS)
Col. Donald M. Dessert, USAF (Ret) (419th NFS)
Paul DiLabbio (6th NFS)
Lt. Col. C. R. "Dick" Ehlert, USAF (Ret) (6th NFS)
John M. Elliott (F2T-1)
Herman E. Ernst (422nd NFS)
Lt. Col. Romeo R. Ferretti, USAF (Ret) (415th NFS)
John E. Florence (6th NFS)
Rolland L. Forrester (421st NFS)
Carl F. Fraser (68th FS)
Russell Glasser (425th NFS)
Robert F. Graham (422nd NFS)
Dale F. Haberman (6th NFS)
Lt. Col. Carl F. Hale, Jr., USAF (Ret) (6th NFS)
Col. Leonard R. Hall, USAF (Ret) (NF Training)
Eugene H. Harris (419th NFS)
Col. William C. Hellriegel, USAF (Ret) (426th NFS)
Philip K. Horrigan (548th NFS)
Jesse H. Jenkins (422nd NFS)
Joe C. Jenkins (414th NFS)
William Jennings (6th and 548th NFS)
Maj. Gen. Oris B. Johnson, USAF (Ret) (422th NFS)
Lt. Col. Frederic J. Kahn, USAF (Ret) (419th NFS)
Brig. Gen. Winston W. Kratz, USAFR (Ret) (NF Training)
Frederick M. Kuykendall, Jr. (548th NFS)
Lt. Col. Laurence W. Lackey, USAF (Ret) (421st NFS)
William M. Laird (422nd NFS)

Col. William A. Larsen, USAF (Ret) (417th NFS)
Bruce K. Leford (548th NFS)
Col. Leon G. Lewis, USAF (Ret) (425th NFS)
Thomas R. Ludlow, Jr. (6th NFS)
Al Lukas (419th NFS)
Richard L. Mathews (547th NFS)
Col. H. A. McCartney, USMC (Ret) (F2T-1)
William G. McKeon (423rd NFS)
Raoul M. Morales (6th NFS)
Col. Paul A. Noel, Jr., USMC (Ret) (F2T-1)
Lt. Col. James A. Null, USAF (Ret) (418th NFS)
Col. William C. Odell, USAF (Ret) (547th NFS)
Lt. Col. John G. Pabst, USAF (Ret) (6th NFS)
Austin G. Petry (415th NFS)
Douglas C. Ponsford (421st NFS)
James F. Postlewaite III (422nd NFS)
Mathias Raab, Jr. (426th NFS)
Col. Phillip A. Rand, USAF (Ret) (419th NFS)
Col. R. L. Rathbun, USMC (F2T-1)
Peter H. Raymen (6th NFS)
James R. Reed (422nd NFS)
L. C. "Duke" Reynolds, Jr. (426th NFS)
William F. Ross (418th NFS)
Prosper F. Rufer (418th NFS)
SMSgt. Robert J. Saddler, USAF (Ret) (4th FS)
W. R. Schrader (425th NFS)
Lt. Col. Kenneth R. Schrieber, USAF (Ret) (547th NFS)
James F. Schroth (419th NFS)
Brig. Gen. M. A. Severson, USMC (Ret) (F2T-1)
Col. Carroll C. Smith, USAF (Ret) (418th NFS)
Paul A. Smith (422nd NFS)
Lt. Karl E. Soukikian (425th NFS)
Lt. Col. Philip R. Teske, USAF (Ret) (6th NFS)
Robert E. Tierney (422nd NFS)
Earl M. Tigner (549th NFS)
Col. Charles M. Townsend, USAF (Ret) (421st NFS)
Lt. Col. Churchill K. Wilcox, USAF (Ret) (422nd NFS)
Porter B. Williamson (NF Training)

Research assistance
Gerald H. Balzer
Dana Bell

Dr. James H. Belote, historian
Dr. William M. Belote, naval historian
Dr. Ira E. Chart, Northrop historian
James V. Crow
James A. Donahue
Lt. Col. William H. Greenhalgh, USAF (Ret)
Ronald C. Harrison
Robert J. Hernandez
Harvey H. Lippincott
Kenn C. Rust, past editor, American Aviation Historical Society Journal
Victoria Stegner
Warren E. Thompson
Louis E. Williams
Jay E. Wright
Air Force Academy Library
Air Force Museum
Albert F. Simpson Historical Research Center
American Aviation Historical Society
Department of the Navy (Office of the Chief of Naval Operations)
Federal Aviation Administration
General Electric Company
Goodyear Aerospace Corporation
Headquarters, US Marine Corps (Historical Branch)
National Aeronautics and Space Administration (Langley, Lewis and Moffett facilities)
National Archives
Naval Air Systems Command
Northrop Corporation and Aircraft Division
Northrop University
Pratt and Whitney Aircraft
Smithsonian Institution and the National Air and Space Museum
United States Air Force (headquarters, command and base historians)
World War II Night Fighters Association

Official USAF Histories
Air Materiel Command History 1946 (Study No. 286)
Army Air Forces School of Applied Tactics
Fighter Command School
Fourth Air Force Historical Study No. I-2
History of the Army Air Forces Technical Training Unit at Northrop Aircraft, Inc., Hawthorne, California
Night Fighter Unit Histories
Project Thunderstorm

Preface

The US Army Air Corps was thrust into the fledgling tactic of night fighting by powers much greater than could be imagined at the time—powers that would reshape the world as it was known. The American military presence in England in 1939 consisted mainly of astute observers of history in the making. The havoc that the Luftwaffe was raining from the night skies was tremendous. But the Royal Air Force's night fighter arm was providing the needed counterpunch. The reports came to the American War Department: develop a night fighter program.

Japanese Adm. Chuichi Nagumo's carrier task force thrust America into the war. Reports of night raids by Japanese aircraft spurred the Air Corps to take the first steps in providing night defense. P-40 Warhawks of the 6th Pursuit Squadron were flown by truly brave men in those dark nights over the Hawaiian Islands in early 1942. They would soon be reequipped with the Douglas P-70 night fighter and be redesignated the 6th Night Fighter Squadron, thus becoming the first operational night fighter squadron in the Army Air Corps.

It was recognized from the beginning that the Air Corps needed a purposely built night fighter. This book tells that story. It was fifty years ago this month that the requirements for what would become the P-61 Black Widow were sent from Wright Field, in Dayton, Ohio, to Northrop Aircraft, in Hawthorne, California. And the story hasn't concluded yet! Capt. Solie Solomon (now Lee Kendall) received an Air Medal for action in the last days of August 1945. It was awarded to him during ceremonies held at March Air Force Base in Riverside, California on Nov. 30, 1990.

The Widow itself is with us even more today. Ten years ago there were only two left—or so most thought. One has been located in China (possibly two more), one in the New Guinea jungles, and rumor has it that another has been located in the wilderness of Alaska.

Although the authors bear full responsibility for the conclusions drawn in this book, their debt to others is considerable. This is their story: the engineers, pilots, radar observers, gunners, maintenance and support personnel. They gave their best efforts, blood and at times, their lives. It is our hope that we have been able to shed some light on these much forgotten warriors.

Chapter 1

Electrical Waves

Airplane technology and the electrically charged world of electronics blossomed during the first forty years of the twentieth century. Conflict has a propensity for escalating technology. The First World War was no different. The powered flying machine broke the barrier of being a fanciful contraption to a real vehicle of flight—the airplane (or aeroplane for our British allies). Though revolutionary at the time, it gave a glimpse of its potential as a war machine.

Development of Radar

Electricity and the various electrical phenomena were in their infancy of being understood by the turn-of-the-century scientists. Such greats as Gustav Hertz, Guglielmo Marconi and Nikola Tesla were quite active in this field of endeavor. How electrical energy traveled through the air was mostly theory. It would be the researchers and scientists in the 1920s and 1930s who, more by accident than not, made the breakthrough discovery. They discovered the ability to detect objects by transmitting electrical impulses in the direction of the object. When the electrical impulses hit an object in their path, the signals are reflected back.

Discovered some time earlier was the fact that these electrical impulses—radio waves—travel at the same speed as light. Thus it was found that the distance between the transmitter and the target could be determined by the time it took the signal to reach the target and return. As this science progressed, its usefulness was first seen as a maritime navigational aid. There were fears expressed at this time that "death rays" were being developed using these same principles. As the 1930s began, the storm clouds of war were rolling over Europe. The sense of impending danger spurred the British to take the lead in this technology, which was called radio direction finding.

As the thirties came to a close, the full storm of war was raging in Europe, and detection of aircraft by the transmission of electrical signals moved into the practical realm. A series of ground stations called chain home (CH) and chain home low (CHL) were set up along the English coast to detect the hoards of incoming Luftwaffe bombers on their mission of destruction. However, more was needed to protect their island and their beloved London.

Night Fighters

Though briefly tried in World War I, the time had come for a more aggressive approach: the art of night fighting. It was realized early on that for the night fighter to have any success, he had to be able to first locate the enemy aircraft. The scenario was soon developed where the ground stations would detect a target and then direct an already airborne night fighter to the vicinity.

Once in the proximity of his intended victim, the night fighter had to accomplish the final phase of detecting the enemy—identifying him as friendly or foe, then destroying him if the latter. Visual sighting was not the optimal method of detection, however. A number of other methods were tried. Radio direction finding (what would soon be known as RADAR) proved to be the most satisfactory method. Being in the heat of battle, though, there was not time to develop an aircraft for the specific purpose of night fighting, so existing fighter and attack aircraft were modified to carry the "black boxes" and pressed into service—and they served well.

Capt. Leonard R. Hall, who was in charge of the radio observers training in the Army Air Force's night fighter school, produced a document entitled *Notes On Night Fighting* which was used as part of the school's training materials. The following short article gives some insight in how the ground radar stations and radar-carrying aircraft worked together based on operations in England.

"The AI (aircraft interception) set is carried in a fighter plane having a seating capacity of at least two. By use of the AI set, the pilot, guided by the AI operator may home directly on the enemy aircraft for the attack. This equipment is purely a defensive weapon.

"The equipment may also be used for *homing on beacons, or for blind landing.*

"The fact that the AI operator is the 'eyes' of the pilot cannot be too strongly stressed.

"There are three types of interceptions carried out. These are as follows:
1. Free-lancing in path of raid.
2. Free-lancing over the target area.
3. Operating in connection with a ground station.

"The first two types of interception, both being free-lancing, have proven to require considerable luck since the coverage is too small.

"The third method by use of the GCI (ground control interception) station is the most satisfactory since the fighter is put on the trail of the bandit by the ground station, at which time the fighter takes over.

"To get the true picture of the tactical setup, it is necessary to go back to the beginning of the interception.

"The CH station (chain home) usually flanked by two CHL stations (chain home low) are stationed around the coast. The CH stations pick up high flying planes while the CHL picks up the lower flying planes. Whenever a plane is picked up, its location by azimuth, range and height is ascertained. This data is transmitted into a filter room. This filter room contains a large map of the area, cross-hatched by grids or squares. As the information is relayed from the CH or CHL stations to the filter room, clerks place small disks on the map according to the grid location received. These disks then show the direction of flight of the 'bandit.' On a small balcony overlooking the map is a group of officers, preferably tactical experts. These officers observe the course of the 'bandit' and communicate with the operations department giving this department information as to the number of interceptor planes to send up, and where to send them. As the 'bandit' approaches inland, the GCI station picks him up. The GCI station is in direct communication with the intercepting aircraft. This station will now plot both the interceptor's path and the 'bandit's' course, meanwhile directing the interceptor so that he will get within range of his AI set. When this range is reached, the command 'Flash your weapon' is given by the GCI station. The interceptor now will turn on his AI set and attempt to pick up the raider. Upon a successful contact with the enemy, the interceptor closes on the tail of the 'bandit' until a 'visual' is obtained by the pilot. 'Tally Ho!' is sounded, meaning the pilot has sighted the enemy and is taking over control of the plane. The pilot then closes and seeks to destroy the enemy. The approved method of approaching is to the rear of the enemy and below him."

Radar Refined

On the other side of the Atlantic, time and circumstances favored American research into this new science. The US Navy had held the lead thus far. Naval researchers coined the term "radio detection and ranging," or radar. The US Army's radar research was carried out mostly at Fort Monmouth near Red Bank, New Jersey, by the Signal Corps, with the Army's Air Corps involvement carried out at Wright Field near Dayton, Ohio.

The war in Europe had a number of influences on the development of radar. Up to this point a number of nations had been carrying out independent research with very little cross-pollination between them. With the arrival of the Tizzard Commission on the North American continent, there was a dramatic change. A formal agenda was laid out, and the United States and Britain each agreed to areas of research they would tackle. Basically, the United States was to take on the promising area of radar that operated in the microwave frequencies.

Though not yet involved in the European fighting, the United States had a number of observers in England. The success of the Royal Air Force's (RAF) fledgling night fighter forces caught the eye of a number of the American observer corps. These reports from overseas, coupled with the research results being obtained in the States, made it evident that the Air Corps needed a night fighter—a designed-for-the-job night fighter. The year was 1939.

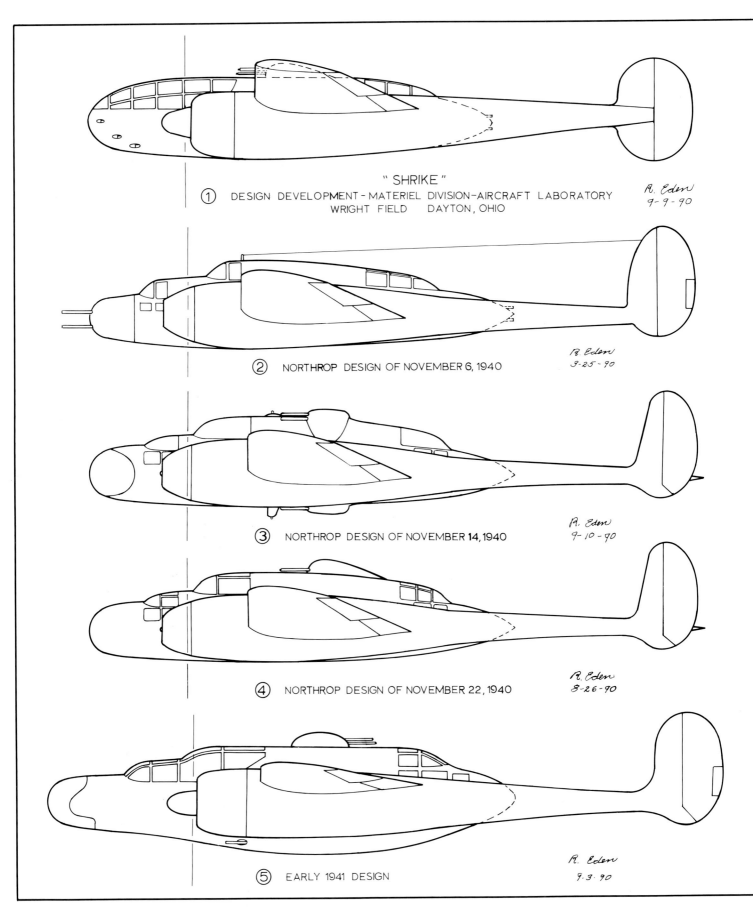

"SHRIKE"
① DESIGN DEVELOPMENT - MATERIEL DIVISION - AIRCRAFT LABORATORY
WRIGHT FIELD   DAYTON, OHIO

R. Eden 9-9-90

② NORTHROP DESIGN OF NOVEMBER 6, 1940

B. Eden 3-25-90

③ NORTHROP DESIGN OF NOVEMBER 14, 1940

R. Eden 9-10-90

④ NORTHROP DESIGN OF NOVEMBER 22, 1940

R. Eden 8-26-90

⑤ EARLY 1941 DESIGN

R. Eden 9-3-90

Chapter 2

Birth of the Black Widow

Jack Northrop had always been a man of foresight. He found little interest in the mundane process of aircraft production. Research and development, the grasping of the future, the striving for the unknown were what stimulated him. It was by this reasoning that he severed his ties with the Douglas Aircraft Co. in 1938. By the summer of the following year, he and a group of associates had formed the Northrop Aircraft Company of Hawthorne, California.

Now Jack Northrop could devote his time and energies to the aircraft of the future, the paramount project being Northrop's dream of an all-wing airplane. The realities of life soon had to be reconciled with, however. Someone, or something, had to pay the bills. This meant some sort of production work.

Subcontract work for portions of aircraft was obtained from such companies as Boeing, Lockheed and Vultee. It was through the latter that Northrop

Development of the initial design. "Shrike," a bird of prey, was a conceptual design of the Design Development Unit of the Materiel Division at Wright Field near Dayton, Ohio, and is shown in the first illustration. This concept could have influenced the Northrop design team (their initial efforts being similar to an improved A-20, but Jack Northrop soon turned them around). On Nov. 6, 1940, Northrop's Pursuit, Night Interceptor resembled the second concept illustrated. This three-man configuration sported ducted spinners and a tail turret. The next iteration was that of a four-man crew with dorsal and ventral turrets. The design in illustration four removes the ventral turret, while illustration five shows a close resemblance to the final XP-61 design. R. M. Eden drawings

had been building A-31 Vengeance dive bombers (a Vultee design) for the Army Air Corps. Now the British desired to purchase the craft, known as the V-72 Vengeance I. Northrop soon purchased the production rights from Vultee to produce these aircraft for the RAF.

It was through this association with the British Purchasing Commission that the subject of a night fighter for the RAF came up. Jack Northrop was involved solely with the design during the initial conversations with the British. Soon he brought in his chief aerodynamicist, Herbert DeCenzo. Northrop outlined the British requirements for a nocturnal fighter for DeCenzo.

Basically, it had to be an airplane that could stop the German night bombing of London. They did not want a fast

At work are Jack Northrop (center), his chief aerodynamicist, Dr. William R. Sears (right) and his assistant chief engineer Walt Cerny (left). Each played an integral role in the development of the P-61. Northrop

Included in the Jan. 30, 1941, contract between Northrop and the Air Corps were two P-61 wind-tunnel models—one at 1/20 scale and the other at 1/30 scale. The 1/20 scale was tested for high speed and control characteristics at Wright Field. The 1/30 scale freespin model was sent to the NACA wind tunnel at Langley, Virginia. Northrop also produced a 1/8 scale model to be used at the California Institute of Technology wind tunnel, and a Zap wing model to be tested at the University of Washington wind tunnel. Thompson-Balzer

scrambler like the Spitfire. They had found that after their speedy aircraft got to the intruder's altitude and started searching for a target, the bombers had already dropped their bombs. Shooting down empty bombers wouldn't accomplish very much, so speed was not a prime attribute. The night fighter had to be able to stay on station above the city of London all night; this meant a total of eight hours loiter time, plus ample fuel to fight. They also specified the armament and the need of a multi-engine design. Sufficient combat altitude to take on the bombers was a must. A requirement to circle at slow speed was also needed.

The United States was quite aware of the 1940 war in Europe and of the plight of its British ally. American military leaders were intensely observing the fighting from both at home and abroad. Among the US air officers in the embattled city of London was Lt. Gen. Delos C. Emmons, who was the commanding general of the General Headquarters Air Force. When he returned to the United States later that year, he included in his report the urgent need for night fighter aircraft. A preliminary specification was drawn up by the Emmons Board and passed to Air Technical Service Command at Wright Field, Ohio, for implementation in late 1940.

Northrop Chief of Research Vladimir H. Pavlecka was at Wright Field on a magnesium wing project at this time—a project that Northrop Aircraft had under subcontract from North American Aviation to design and produce—assisting on the testing. Pavlecka, who had no knowledge of either Northrop's night fighter talks with the British or of the USAAC's interests, was called into Col. Lawrence C. Craigie's office (Chief, Experimental Aircraft Projects) on October 21, 1940. They had never met before. Craigie's first words to Pavlecka were, "Now sit down. Don't take any notes. Just try to keep this in your memory!"

The craft that was then outlined to the somewhat startled Northrop engineer was an airplane that was to fly at night. He was told nothing about radar, except that there was a way to see and to distinguish other airplanes. He was also told that it had to be a twin-engine plane, manned by a pilot and an operator of the device that would locate aircraft in the dark, and the armament requirements. After being made to repeat the instructions several times to ensure their retention, he was sent packing and placed on a night flight for Los Angeles.

The next morning, October 22, Jack Northrop met with Pavlecka and received the Air Corps specifications. The injunction from the Air Corps did not inquire if Northrop Aircraft *could* do it; they were ordered to do it! Neither Northrop nor Pavlecka was aware of any other company designing a night fighter at this time; though, it was in this time frame that Douglas started on their XA-26A night fighter (the AAC were considering the A-20B as an interim night fighter at this time). With a minimum amount of rework to his British night fighter, Northrop was ready to present a night fighter design to the Air Corps. On November 5, he and Assistant Chief Engineer Walter J. Cerny left for Wright Field.

Design Specifications

At Wright Field, Northrop and Cerny met with Materiel Command and the many associated laboratory representatives. The aircraft Northrop presented was to be powered by two of the new Pratt and Whitney Double-Wasp R-2800 engines mounted in low-slung nacelles. They tapered back into twin tail booms which were connected by a large horizontal stabilizer and elevator. The long fuselage, which projected fore and aft of the inner wing panels, housed the crew of three. The crew consisted of a gunner for the nose turret, a pilot and a radar operator/rear turret gunner. Each turret held four .50 caliber machine guns.

Dimensionally, the craft had an overall height of 13 ft. 2 in., was 45 ft. 6 in. long and had a wingspan of 66 ft. The landing gear for this bomber-size fighter were of the tricycle configuration with a wheelbase of 160 in. For short field takeoffs and landings, it had Zap flaps spanning 140 in. along the trailing edge of its wing. Empty weight was 16,245 lb. and its gross weight was 22,654 lb.

Many lengthy discussions followed Northrop's initial presentation. The making of the Air Corps' Night Interceptor Pursuit airplane was on its way.

The Northrop party returned to California to put these new concepts into an engineered design. An interim

On Apr. 2, 1941, representatives from the General Headquarters, Air Force, Wright Field, US Navy, the National Defense Research Council and the British Air Commission viewed the mock-up at the Northrop plant in Hawthorne, California. A major change after the mock-up was moving the 20 mm cannon from the outboard portion of the wing to the lower portion of the crew nacelle. Northrop via Balzer

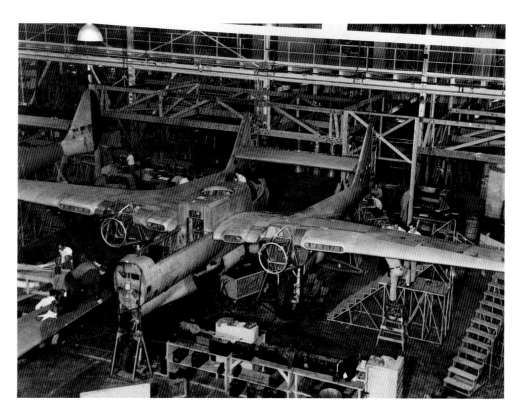

The production of two prototypes were ordered by the Air Corps in the original contract with Northrop on Jan. 30, 1942. Just thirty-eight days later, thirteen service test (Y) aircraft and a static test airframe (no engines nor instruments) were ordered. Shown under construction is the static test article (c/n 703). Northrop via Balzer

Test pilot John Myers and unidentified flight-test engineer taxi out XP-61 Number 1 for a day's flight-test activity. Though some of the flight testing originated out of Northrop Field near Hawthorne, California, and actually was conducted off the California coast over the Pacific, much of the experimental flight testing, and later production aircraft testing, was conducted from the Ontario, California, airport. The Ontario area did not have the population density of the Hawthorne area, thus was safer for this type of work. Northrop via Balzer

Most of the first XP-61's flying was in support of flight testing conducted in California. The second XP-61 first flew on Nov. 18, 1941, and participated in the test flying activities in California until Apr. 15, 1943. Major Marshall Roth flew it from Ontario, California, to Wright Field, a flight of 8.3 hours. It was shortly after its arrival at Wright Field that the Aircraft Radio Laboratory installed AI radar in the plane for the first time. Upon visiting Wright Field, Gen.

Henry H. "Hap" Arnold, chief of Army Air Corps, asked: "Who is responsible for this assortment of built-in head winds?" Maj. Gen. Oliver P. Echols, commanding general of Materiel Command, who was accompanying General Arnold, announced proudly that the speed tests conducted to date demonstrated the XP-61's ability to meet, and actually exceed by 1 mph, the Northrop guaranteed performance. USN via National Archives

configuration of a single-tail, shoulder-high wing design was contemplated for a short time, then discarded. This design resembled an A–20 with R–2800 engines. By November 14, Northrop presented this revised design to the Air Corps. This new version had an additional gunner's station. Nose and tail turrets of the original design were replaced by a twin .50 caliber machine gun in the belly, and four .50 caliber machine guns in a dorsal turret. The crew composition was now two gunners, a pilot and a radar operator. The airborne intercept radar was now located in the craft's nose, and the fabrication of this area was composed of a nonmetal material.

Additional refinements were to be made as a result of another round of talks with Wright Field personnel. A further modified design was ready by November 22. Once again the crew was of a three-man configuration—pilot, gunner and radar operator. The armament also changed again. Four 20 mm cannons were located in the wings. The lower belly turret had been deleted, but the top turret was retained. The wheelbase had been broadened to 172 in., and the gross weight was reduced to 21,839 lb. This was formalized into Northrop Specification 8A (or NS–8A) dated Dec. 5, 1940.

NS–8A was submitted to Wright Field for their evaluation. When the comments of the various Wright Field laboratories were received, Northrop and his engineers once again revised their design into what became Change A to NS–8A, dated Dec. 16, 1940. With changed specification in hand, Jack Northrop journeyed, again, to Dayton. This new change met all the requirements of those concerned. A letter of quotation was prepared by Northrop for two experimental airplanes. It was submitted to Materiel Command on December 17, and an Authority for Purchase was issued that day. Northrop Aircraft signed the formal contract the following Jan. 11, 1941, and forwarded it to Washington, DC, where it was recommended for approval on January 29 by the assistant chief of the Army Air Forces and approved the following day by the undersecretary of war.

XP-61 and YP-61

A $1,367,000 contract was let to Northrop by the Air Corps on Jan. 30,

1941, for two experimental airplanes and two wind-tunnel models—one at 1/20 scale and the other at 1/30 scale. The 1/20 scale wind-tunnel model was for testing at Wright Field where high-speed and control characteristics tests were to be performed. The 1/30 scale freespin model was to be sent to the National Advisory Committee for Aeronautics (NACA) wind tunnel at Langley, Virginia. Though not included in the contract, Northrop would fabricate two additional models— a 1/8 scale model which would be used at the California Institute of Technology wind tunnel, and a Zap wing model to be tested at the University of Washington wind tunnel.

During this period, Edward Zap was working with Northrop Aircraft on an NACA contract. Numerous Northrop personnel were assisting Zap in a number of the experiments concerning control characteristics using different types of spoilers and aileron configurations. Incorporated in the Northrop night fighter design was the Zap wing and Zap flap. Since the mid- to late 1930s, Zap experimented with increasing the maximum lift coefficient and consequent decreased landing speed by the use of new and improved lateral control and lifting devices, which became known as Zap flaps and Zap circular-type ailerons. The XP-61 of January 1941 was designed with the Zap wing and Zap flap but did not employ any type of circular arc, spoiler-type aileron.

Gen. Carl Spaatz, chief of the Materiel Division of the Air Corps, and Lt. Col. Frank Hunter went to Wright Field in late February 1941 to effect final coordination with the Experimental Engineering Section on all points of the military characteristics of the XP-61. It was during this visit that discussions of a contract for thirteen YP-61 service test aircraft were initiated. Both Spaatz and Hunter knew well of the urgent need of a night fighter from their stay in England during the fall of 1940. There they had witnessed the devastating effects of the Luftwaffe's night assault upon London. Jack Northrop submitted his bid, along with specification NS-8B, for the service test aircraft on February 8. By March 10, 1941, some thirty-eight days after the approval of the XP-61 contract, the undersecretary of war approved a contract worth over $5.5 million to finance the construction of thirteen YP-61 Night

Interceptor Pursuit airplanes, plus one engineless static test airframe. (Unlike the XP-61 experimental airplane, the YP-61 service test aircraft would be flown by operational test organizations and training units, and would perform special tests such as cold-weather operation testing.) These aircraft were to be identical to the XP-61s then being tested.

Northrop's night fighter was experiencing its share of delays and setbacks, a phenomenon not unusual with a piece of equipment pushing the state of the art. The first major obstacle was encountered in March 1941, when the Army-Navy Standardization Committee decided to standardize on updraft carburetion for the aircraft's engines. This caused a great deal of anxiety at Northrop, because their design used a downdraft system. Changing to the updraft system would have caused approximately seventy-five percent scrappage of the work already completed, which would lead to a two-month slippage in schedule. But on the twenty-first of the month, the Committee reversed its decision, causing much jubilation at Northrop.

April 2 found the mock-up board convened at the Northrop plant in Hawthorne, California. Representatives from the General Headquarters Air Force, Wright Field, the US Navy, the National Defense Research Council and the British Air Commission were in attendance.

In general, they found the mock-up acceptable, though there were a number of changes that they felt were mandatory. The greatest of these was the removal of the four 20 mm cannons from the wings of the aircraft to its belly. There were two major advantages to this change. First was ease of maintenance, and second was better airflow over the wings (improved aerodynamic characteristics). The board felt that the relocation of the armor plates would provide better protection for the crew and ammunition boxes. They also recommended the installation of flame arresters for the engine exhausts to help conceal the aircraft's presence in the night sky. Last, the redistribution of certain radio equipment was also advised.

These changes meant many hours of reengineering, more tests and evaluations, which would add up to about thirty days slippage in schedule and a cost increase of more than $38,000. Greater range than that predicted from initial calculations was recommended by Materiel Command in February. To accommodate this, the aircraft's internal fuel capacity had been increased from 540 gallons in two tanks to 646 gallons in four self-sealed tanks built into the wings. This design change was approved February 28. This was not the end, however, for in early March, Wright Field initiated investigations into in-

This XP-61-NO, serial number 41-119509, was the first of its kind built. It has the early-design smooth canopy and flat-black paint scheme. It bears the earlier national insig-

nia. Both XP models would have the flat-black paint removed, and would finish out their days in natural metal finish. Tinker Air Force Base

First flight of the XP-61 took place on May 26, 1942, with contract test pilot Vance Breese at the controls. In a June 1942 memo for the Director of Military Requirements, Brig. Gen. B. E. Meyers quotes Breese as stating that the XP-61 "...flies beautifully and is an old man's airplane." Also of interest in this memo is Meyers' discussion of needed production capability of 140 P-61s a month! Following the first flight, a number of design changes were incorporated. The horizontal stabilizer and elevator were redesigned to give the plane improved longitudinal stability. The Zap flaps were replaced by full-span flaps, which required redesign of the entire trailing edge of the wings. The standard ailerons were replaced by circular, retractable ailerons. These changes were authorized by the Army Air Corps and incorporated in the plane by year's end. Northrop via Balzer

creasing the internal fuel capacity to even greater amounts. The possibility of hanging external fuel tanks onto the aircraft was also discussed.

A two-stage, two-speed, intercooled, mechanical supercharger was part of the R-2800 powerplant designated for the P-61 as initially designed for the Air Corps. The thinking in some circles was that the added weight and complexity of a turbosupercharger installation was not necessary. This line of reasoning was not accepted by all at Northrop, where such designers as Dr. William R. Sears, Irving L. Ashkenas and John M. Wild felt that the extra horsepower the turbosupercharger provided was necessary. As it turned out, the anti-turbosupercharger forces prevailed.

The twin boom idea was not merely a copy of Lockheed's P-38. This arrangement was an original part of the night-fighting concept, influenced, not required, by the British during their discussions with Northrop. Night-fighting combat was to be a head-to-tail affair. The pursuing aircraft would have to close in on the enemy aircraft and stay in the pursued aircraft's slipstream while trying to make positive identification before shooting it down. The twin rudders were considered to give greater stability in such circumstances.

For night fighting, the greater the visibility from the cockpit and the more eyes that could scan the skies, the better. The P-61's "stepped up" canopy provided a clear field of vision for the gunner. Likewise, the rear fuselage with its clear tail cone gave the radar operator (R/O) a good rearward view, which enabled him to act as a tail gunner if attacked from astern.

Tricycle landing gear, a fairly new innovation, was employed to give this bomber-sized fighter better ground handling characteristics. Aircraft equipped with conventional gear demanded greater pilot control and attention on takeoff and landing. The better forward visibility and ease of handling provided by the tricycle gear on the P-61 proved to be a joy for its pilots.

Airborne Interception Radar

Radar is an important part of the night fighter story and an integral part of the aircraft that performed the night fighter mission. The type of radar used in night fighter aircraft was called AI, an acronym meaning Aircraft Interception or Airborne Interception (the name changed as the war progressed). A modified Army SCR-268 Searchlight Controller Radar was the Air Corps' first AI radar to fly. The set was modified at the Signal Corps Laboratories, Fort Monmouth, New Jersey, in early 1941 and was installed in a B-18A at nearby Red Bank airport. (British experimental AI equipment was in operation as early as June 1939. A demonstration for the chief of the RAF's Fighter Command took place in August of that year.)

It was from a suggestion of the British Mission that the National Defense Research Committee's (NDRC) Microwave Committee decided to establish a development laboratory to undertake the development of microwave aircraft-interception equipment and microwave position-finder equipment for antiaircraft fire control. The Massachusetts Institute of Technology (MIT) was persuaded to be the responsible administration authority for the Radiation Laboratory. Under the guidance of Dr. L. A. DuBridge, the laboratory became active in early November 1940.

By June 18, 1941, NDRC's Radiation Laboratory had completed its preliminary development work on the Black Widow's AI radar—designated AI-10. At this time the Radiation Lab had started its production efforts on thirty such sets (by now given the military designation of SCR-520). Fifteen of the sets were scheduled for the XP- and YP-61s and one for Western Electric Company, which was to refine the design and mass-produce the set.

Plans for installing Western Electric production radar in lieu of the experimental sets would be made the following January 9. This change in thinking was based on the experimental nature of the MIT equipment and the desirability of having the same sets as the production aircraft.

Construction of the two XP-61 aircraft proceeded at a constant rate through the summer months of 1941. During this time additional changes were deliberated, of which two were

A rear view of the Pratt & Whitney R-2800-25S, which originally powered the XP-61. After experiencing numerous engine failures, Pratt & Whitney, the engine manufacturer, was brought in by Northrop to investigate the problem. It was found that the root cause of the failures was oil and gas being trapped in the engine's crankcase. Because of the severity of the problem, and to minimize flight schedule impact, the XP-61 was grounded in July while R-2800-10 engines were installed in lieu of the –25S. Balzer

19

During August and September 1943 the thirteen YP-61s were completed. Their assignments would be varied. Some would stay at Northrop for flight testing and factory training of maintenance personnel, some would go to Wright and Patterson fields in Ohio for accelerated service test and radio mock-up tests. Others went to Florida where they would perform operational suitability tests under the AAF's Proving Ground Command, and flight and armament tests by both the Proving Ground Command and the AAF's School of Applied Tactics. In addition, the YP-61 would support the fledgling night fighter training program. National Archives

approved in October of that year. Of major importance was a change approved in mid-month for the installation of a pedestal-type mount for the turret guns, instead of the General Electric ring-type mount. Northrop asked approval for the change due to difficulties they were encountering in attempting to install the original mount.

During that same month, it also became apparent that General Electric would not be able to supply the turret prior to first flight.

The P-61 program was under priority A-1-B, the standard priority for experimental aircraft. The War Department would have to change the priority to A-1-A to enable Northrop to obtain a scarce wartime item such as the General Electric turret. This was not possible because of greater needs of existing production aircraft. So it was decided to install a mock-up turret for flight-test purposes to prevent additional delays. Another problem cropped up in February 1942. The Curtiss propellers originally called for in the design specifica-

tions for the production aircraft would not be available. Again, improvise or perish was the word of the day. Hamilton Standard propellers were tried during the XP-61's flight test and found to be unsatisfactory, primarily due to severe vibrations caused by the engine-propeller combination. Northrop attempted to correct this condition but was unsuccessful. Fortunately, the Curtiss propellers once again became available prior to the completion of the production aircraft.

Test Flight of the XP-61 and YP-61

May 26, 1942, was a day long awaited. At 4:37 pm, veteran contract test pilot Vance Breese lifted the 30,000 lb. giant off the Northrop Field runway. (Actually, an inadvertent liftoff had taken place on May 21 during ground runs.) It had been rumored that Breese received $1,000 per foot of wingspan for the test flight, which would have been $66,000 for the Widow. The performance of the craft during its brief fifteen-minute sojourn through the blue south-

ern California sky far exceeded the hopes of its designers. After landing, Breese climbed out of the big, flat-black bird, walked over to Northrop and said, "Jack, you've got a damn fine airplane!"

Building unique experimental models and production manufacturing can be (and usually is) quite different. The production line found the tolerances for the Zap flaps too critical and beyond the feasibility of then-current production processes. The entire outer wing section aft of the main spar was redesigned. Full-span, conventional slotted flaps were installed in the outer wing's edge while the inner wing sections retained the Zap flaps.

In mid-June 1942, Northrop started investigations into improving the Black Widow's longitudinal stability. A new horizontal tail was designed that would complement the aerodynamic characteristics of the recently installed full-span flaps. The new configuration was test flown in July. The changes brought about improved flight characteristics, except for those periods when the Zap flaps were extended. More changes to the trailing edge of the wing brought about the complete elimination of the Zap flap and the addition of the spoiler-type aileron (in addition to the conventional ailerons).

The spoilers were curved, perforated magnesium structures located in the rear one-third of the wing. Combined with the conventional ailerons, they produced the desired rolling moment at speeds even below the stall speed. The total area in the fully raised position was 11.45 sq-ft. The conventional ailerons were primarily for peace of mind for the pilots who had been used to conventional ailerons; they simply provided the feel of ailerons to the pilot. It was believed by some Army pilots that the spoiler ailerons would not function when the aircraft was in inverted flight. Their fears were quickly dispelled, however, when Northrop test pilot John Myers put the Widow through its paces, including beautifully executed slow rolls. This new control system vastly improved direction stability at low speeds, even below stall speed and with one prop feathered—an almost unprecedented feat of aerodynamics.

The name Black Widow *adorns this YP–61–NO, serial number 41–18887. You can see the* three-man crew, with each at his station in this aerial view.

To reduce vibration from firing the .50 caliber turret guns, some YP–61s were equipped with only two turret guns. Northrop

Chapter 3

Warrior Craft

The Japanese attack on Pearl Harbor on Dec. 7, 1941, brought the United States into war and hastened the development of the P-61. A Letter of Intent was initiated on December 24 which called for 100 P-61 series airplanes and spare parts. This order covered aircraft under Northrop Specification 8C Night Interceptor Pursuit, Air Corps Model P-61 (July 15, 1941). This change, dated Dec. 1, 1941, became the specification for the YP series service test aircraft and all P-61A models. It was amended some three weeks later when Supplement 1, dated Jan. 17, 1942, authorized construction of an additional fifty aircraft.

A second supplement superseded the previous Letter of Intent and Supplement Agreement. This production contract ordered 410 aircraft. Fifty aircraft were called for under the Second Lend Lease Program as Pursuit, Fighter two-engine Northrop, Hawthorne, P-61, and were covered by RFDA No. 7205, Project 112 (Contract DAW 535 AC-1044). As many as 360 aircraft were ordered for the US Army Air Corps (Contract W 535 AC-21061).

Under these contracts, $7.1 million was chargeable to Defense Aide, and $55.7 million to Air Corps Appropriations. The delivery schedule called for twelve aircraft to be delivered in April 1943 to the RAF under Lend Lease, with an additional thirty-eight in May. The Air Corps were to get their first seven in

May, forty-five more aircraft between June and December 1943 and a further thirty-eight to be delivered in January 1944.

P-61 Variants

In the heat of the early days of the war, the need for a great number of P-61s was foreseen. On May 25 an agreement was reached between Northrop and the Air Corps to produce 1,200 Widows from a government facility in Denver, Colorado. By the end of July 1942 that number was cut down to

207 aircraft, and the Northrop production facilities in Hawthorne, California, were to be used.

P-61A

When the first P-61A-1 rolled off the production line in October 1943, the Lend Lease order for RAF P-61s was no longer on the schedule. Externally, the P-61A-1's outline differed from the experimental and service test P-61s in the construction of the pilot's and gunner's canopy. Weaknesses found in the YP series during flight testing brought about a strengthened structure in the produc-

A view of the Widow testing its firepower. It gives a feeling of the fearsome sight seen by any enemy plane whose misfortune it was to become the prey of the Widow in the night skies. Wolford

This P–61A–1–NO was one of the earliest of the Widows produced for actual service. It was painted in olive drab over gray, which would be the standard color of the P–61A–1s

and 5s. The later models would be painted glossy black. This aircraft, serial number 42–5495, was also among the 37A models to have the top turret.

Northrop test pilots (from left) John Myers, Max Stanley, Harry Crosby and Alex Popona. Attorney turned test pilot and then aviation executive, Myers not only tested the Widow but traveled to the combat areas of the central and southwest Pacific to assist the night fighter crews who had the double duty of flying combat missions and transitioning into a new aircraft that they hadn't flown in before. Once that not-so-small task was accomplished, he gave a helping hand to the night fighter training organization back in the States. Stanley, who is probably better known for his flying wing flights, had two hair-raising flights while testing the fighter brake concept that would become part of the P-61C. Northrop

tion variants. This strengthening eliminated the smooth flow of the earlier Widow's greenhouse and created sharper, more abrupt changes in angle in that area for the production craft. The welded magnesium alloy booms of the earlier aircraft were extremely difficult to manufacture and posed great quality control problems. For these reasons, the production aircraft's booms were fabricated from aluminum alloy. Unlike the earlier planes, which were painted flat black, the A models were adorned with olive drab upper and gray lower surfaces.

Armament consisted of four 20 mm cannons in the belly, but only the first thirty-seven of the forty-five P-61A-1s produced were equipped with dorsal turrets. There were two major reasons for the deletion of the turret from more than half of the P-61s produced. First, the turrets caused a buffeting problem. The buffeting occurred when the turret was either elevated and/or rotated in azimuth while in flight. Though Northrop would spend many flight-test hours in trying to eliminate this problem, it was never completely eliminated. The second factor leading to the elimination of the turret was a more urgent need for it on other aircraft (mainly the B-29 program).

The first of the P-61A-1s weighed 29,240 lb. empty. With the dorsal turret deleted, the aircraft weighed 27,600 lb.

An aerial view of P-61A-1-NO, serial number 42-5507. It was one of the earlier models and had the top turret. Wolford

It is of interest to note that with a reduction of over 1,600 lb., the top speed of the aircraft was increased only by 3 mph.

Despite its size, the P-61 proved to be quite docile. Its flight characteristics were excellent. Full control of the aircraft could be maintained with one engine out when fully loaded. A unique feature of this plane was its ability to be slow rolled into a dead engine, and for the pilot to be in full control at all times.

The first P-61A-1 to go overseas was serial number 42-5496. Its destination was not a combat zone, but for test and evaluation by the RAF in England. This Widow was in English hands between Mar. 21, 1944, and Feb. 22, 1945, when it was returned to the AAF. The RAF was not too enthusiastic about the plane's performance, however.

Most of the A-1 models went to AAF night fighter squadrons (NFS) in the

Pacific. First to receive this craft was the oldest operational AAF night fighter squadron, the 6th, then stationed in the Hawaiian Islands. Two days later, on May 3, 1944, the 419th NFS on Guadalcanal was the second squadron to turn in its makeshift P-70 and P-38 night-fighting planes for the Widow.

A change in designation to P-61A-5 began with the forty-sixth P-61 produced. The 2,250 hp R-2800-65 engines

This line-up of P-61A-5-NOs is painted olive drab over gray. They were the first to *replace the 2,000 hp R-2800-10 with the 2,250 hp R-2800-65. Most of these aircraft* *were sent to the 422nd and 425th squadrons stationed in Europe.* Wolford

The pilot's "office." The square hole in the instrument panel is where the pilot's radar scope is to be installed. Most photos of this era do not show the scope because of its classified nature. Balzer replaced the 2,000 hp R-2800-10s. The P-61A-5s carried the same olive-drab-over-gray paint scheme as the A-1s. Most of these aircraft were sent across the Atlantic where they equipped the Ninth Air Force's 422nd and 425th night fighter squadrons in late May and early June 1944, respectively.

The last major A change was the P-61A-10 that incorporated water injection with its R-2800-65 Double-Wasp engines. The most visible external feature of this series was its shiny-black paint job. Of the 120 P-61A-10s produced, twenty were modified prior to delivery by the addition of a pylon on the outer wing panels. Initially, these pylons were to carry either 165 gallon auxiliary fuel tanks (later 310 gallon tanks were installed) or 1,600 lb. bombs. These planes were redesignated P-61A-11.

P-61B

The next major P-61 variant was the B model (per NS-8D). The major change that brought about this change in model designation was the replacement of the SCR-720A AI radar by the improved C model.

Externally, the P-61B series differed from that of the A in an 8 in. longer crew nacelle and split main landing-gear doors. The most apparent difference between the P-61A and P-61B is the access panel added behind the radome on the P-61B.

Changes took place in the landing-gear system also. Externally, one of

In this once-restricted photo, we are allowed to see the pilot's radar scope installed. Northrop

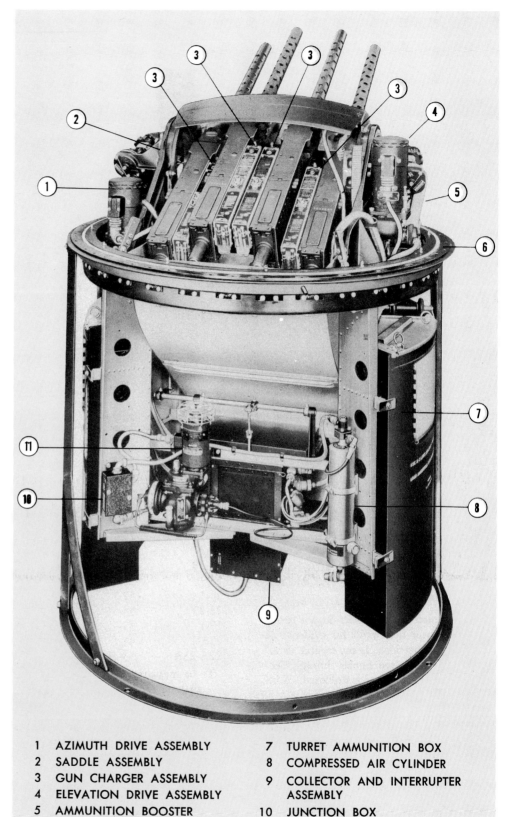

The turret assembly diagram from an AAF manual. Northrop

1	AZIMUTH DRIVE ASSEMBLY	7	TURRET AMMUNITION BOX
2	SADDLE ASSEMBLY	8	COMPRESSED AIR CYLINDER
3	GUN CHARGER ASSEMBLY	9	COLLECTOR AND INTERRUPTER ASSEMBLY
4	ELEVATION DRIVE ASSEMBLY		
5	AMMUNITION BOOSTER	10	JUNCTION BOX
6	RING ASSEMBLY	11	COMPRESSOR

The gunner's compartment, just behind and above the pilot. The gunner's sighting station is shown in the down position. Balzer

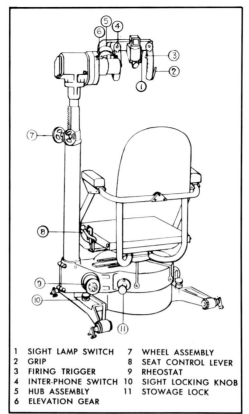

1	SIGHT LAMP SWITCH	7	WHEEL ASSEMBLY
2	GRIP	8	SEAT CONTROL LEVER
3	FIRING TRIGGER	9	RHEOSTAT
4	INTER-PHONE SWITCH	10	SIGHT LOCKING KNOB
5	HUB ASSEMBLY	11	STOWAGE LOCK
6	ELEVATION GEAR		

This diagram from an AAF manual identifies the P-61's sighting equipment. Northrop

This aerial view of an early olive-drab-over-gray P-61A provides an excellent view of the four 20 mm cannons in the belly. Wolford

28

previous page
With 120 produced, the P–61A–10 was the most numerous version of the A model. Besides being the first variant to get the gloss-black paint scheme, the major change in the 10 series was the incorporation of water injection with its R–2800–65 Double-Wasp radial engines. Twenty were modified prior to delivery to operational units with the addition of pylons on the outboard wings, which enabled them to carry more fuel in external tanks, or more ordnance. With the pylons, 165 gallon external fuel tanks were originally attached to give the Widow either extended range or longer loiter time. Later, tanks as large as 310 gallons were attached. Bombs up to 1,000 lb. and rocket launchers of various configurations were also attached. These aircraft were redesignated P–61A–11. Northrop

these changes is quite apparent in the construction of the main-gear doors. In the P–61B series aircraft they were of a split configuration. This change allowed the aft three quarters of the doors to close again after the gear had been extended, preventing mud, rocks and miscellaneous objects from being thrown up into the wheelwells by the tires. Other changes to the landing gear included the replacement of the A model's hydraulically operated main landing-gear doors by mechanical ones, addition of a main-gear down-lock emergency release which allowed the pilot to release the locks in an emergency (even if the entire hydraulic system was out), and a safety latch on the main-gear hydraulic valve handle to eliminate possible retraction of the gear while on the ground.

Experiments at the night fighter training school in Florida, along with suggestions from the field, brought about the inclusion of night binoculars in the B model for the pilot. These were a combination of 5.8 power night glasses and an optical gunsight. In place of the circle and dot of light in his regular gunsight, there was a horizontal row of four illuminated dots in the gunsight of the binoculars. The pilot lined up these dots with the wing of the aircraft he was tracking, and used this combination for an artificial horizon. This enabled the pilot to determine his prey's range with remark-

A flock of later-model P–61As on the Northrop field. Northrop

A beautiful shot of a Black Widow frolicking in the clouds. The lighting of the sun from above illuminates the stiffeners in the R/O's clear plexiglass tail cone. Earlier models without this enforcement experienced implosion during high-speed dives. Northrop via Balzer

able accuracy. A number of the later A models produced were retrofitted with night binoculars in the field and at Air Force modification centers.

Like the P-61A-11s, some B models were equipped with the wing racks for up to 310 gallon fuel tanks or 1,600 lb. bombs. Aircraft in Blocks 1 and 5 car-ried no racks while those in blocks 10, 15, 20 and 25 were equipped with four wing-rack stations. Other P-61Bs were modified in the field or at modification

The B model was quite different from the A. The nose was lengthened for the upgraded SCR-720C AI radar; the rectangular inspec-tion panel just aft of the nose cone/forward fuselage separation line is a real giveaway. Split main landing-gear doors were incor-porated to protect the wheelwell from debris picked up by the tires. Both the operational crews in the combat theaters and the night fighter organization in the States deter-mined that the pilot needed to have night binoculars. The B model incorporated them. The P-61B-15 was the first variant to rein-troduce the turret in the Black Widow line. Though one of the major reasons for deleting the turret in the first place was a vibration problem when the guns were fired, the real reason seems to be the turret having higher priorities in other aircraft programs. The combat crews that flew the early P-61s with the turret didn't have any problem in their operation. Northrop

centers to carry two wing racks. These aircraft were given intermediate numbers of P-61B-2, 6, 11 and 16.

Other changes incorporated in the P-61B series included a bigger and better heater system for the crew, automatically operated lower engine-cowl flaps, oil-cooler air exit flaps and intercooler flaps; oil tanks in the engine nacelles instead of the outer wings; a taxi lamp added to the landing-gear strut; the aileron trim tabs were deleted (this was due to the excellent lateral control given by the retractable aileron system); and a built-in fire extinguisher system was added.

Major changes in the differing block numbers within the B model series included replacing the SCR-718 radio altimeter with an APN-1 low-altitude altimeter starting with the P-61B-5 series. An APS-13 tail warning system was added to the P-61B-10 planes. Some late model As and early Bs were modified in the field or retrofitted at either the Northrop production facilities or at AAF modification centers with the APN-1 and APS-13. The P-61B-15 brought back the dorsal turret (Type A-4) and the P-61B-20 used the Type A-7 turret. Both were General Electric turrets.

The last variant of the B model series was the P-61B-25. There were only seven of these aircraft in total, and the project was completely experimental in nature. In these aircraft the standard SCR-720 AI radar was replaced with Western Electric APG-1 gun-laying radar which was coupled to a General Electric remote-control turret system

An excellent view of the SCR-720 radar unit is provided as radar technician Sergeant Papavich inspects the unit in Skippy, *a P-61 flown by the 421st NFS. The photo was taken Nov. 2, 1944, during the four months the 421st was stationed at Tacloban, Leyte. US Army*

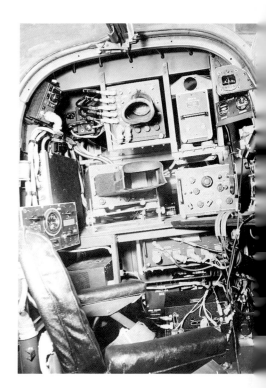

The R/O station in a P-61B. In the upper right-hand corner is a compass. Below the compass, from left to right, is the blinker and oxygen gauge. In the center top is the azimuth radar scope assembly, and below is the horizon radar scope. Bob Hughes via Warren Thompson

The assembly line of Department 53 at Northrop is lined with P-61Bs in production.

Note the oxygen bottles installed in the engine nacelles. Northrop

(both models 2CRT12C2 and 2CFR12C3 were used). Through this arrangement the computer aimed the guns according to data received from the radar. One P-61B-15 was so configured for test purposes. Apparently, the AAF felt further expenditures were warranted, so the first six P-61B-20 series were also modified.

Sterling C. Walter was one of the Northrop people responsible for these aircraft. Walter said, "Originally there were ten aircraft to be produced. They were completed aircraft. We had to remove all of the wires and rewire them, about five miles worth. 110 VAC generators were installed (possibly the first aircraft to have these)." The main differ-

ence between the two remote-control turret systems used on this project was that the 2CFR12C3 included a Model 2CH2A3 "mechanical" computer. For the most part these aircraft saw service with the Air Proving Command at Eglin Field, Florida, and at the night fighter training establishment at Hammer Field, California.

With Old Glory flying over the work stations, these P-61Bs are being completed by the *workers of departments 18 and 53 at Northrop.* Northrop

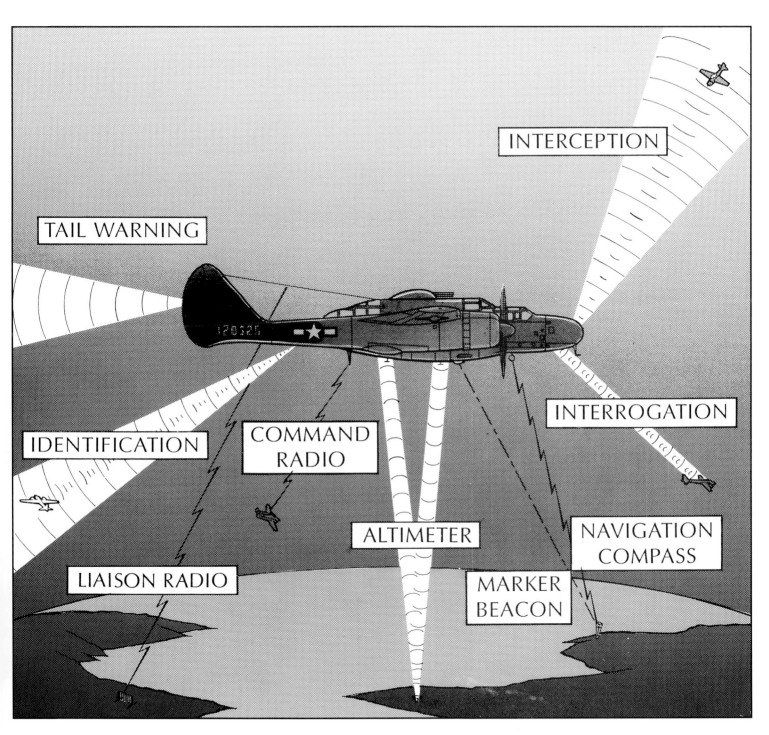

TAIL WARNING

INTERCEPTION

IDENTIFICATION

COMMAND RADIO

INTERROGATION

LIAISON RADIO

ALTIMETER

NAVIGATION COMPASS

MARKER BEACON

The P–61 Black Widow was equipped with five radar devices—interception, interrogation, altimeter, identification and tail warning. These served the Widow well as five senses for night fighting. This is a recreation by Jack Moses of a diagram published in Northrop News, Dec. 3, 1947.

Northrop technicians check over a P–61B before a flight. Northrop

Dimensions of the
NORTHROP
BLACK WIDOW P-61

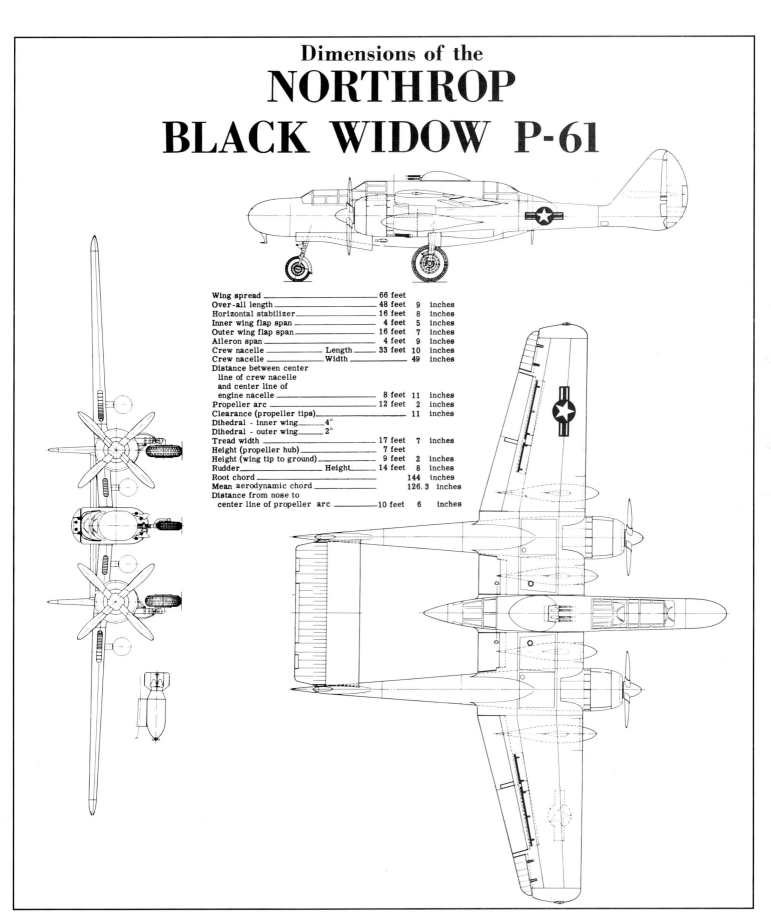

Wing spread		66 feet	
Over-all length		48 feet	9 inches
Horizontal stabilizer		16 feet	8 inches
Inner wing flap span		4 feet	5 inches
Outer wing flap span		16 feet	7 inches
Aileron span		4 feet	9 inches
Crew nacelle	Length	33 feet	10 inches
Crew nacelle	Width		49 inches
Distance between center line of crew nacelle and center line of engine nacelle		8 feet	11 inches
Propeller arc		12 feet	2 inches
Clearance (propeller tips)			11 inches
Dihedral - inner wing	4°		
Dihedral - outer wing	2°		
Tread width		17 feet	7 inches
Height (propeller hub)		7 feet	
Height (wing tip to ground)		9 feet	2 inches
Rudder	Height	14 feet	8 inches
Root chord			144 inches
Mean aerodynamic chord			126.3 inches
Distance from nose to center line of propeller arc		10 feet	6 inches

Chapter 4

Battlefield Florida

Army Air Forces (AAF) night fighter tactics development and training can find its origins in the reorganization of the War Department in March 1942. Under this new organizational scheme, the reconstituted AAF staff included a director of Air Defense. Taking the helm as director was Col. Gordon P. Saville. Colonel Saville was well qualified for this position. He had served earlier in the Air Defense Command, and had been one of the US military observers in the British

Lt. Col. Winston W. Kratz with an RAF Spitfire VB at Bovingdon, England, in January 1942. Bovingdon was a bomber station but because it was the closest to VIII FC headquarters at Watford, it was frequented by VIII FC personnel such as Kratz on a regular basis. It was through Kratz' interest and association with night fighter operations while with VIII FC that he became head of the AAF's night fighter program when he returned to the United States in May 1942. Kratz

Isles prior to America's entry into hostilities.

Recognizing the need for air defense training and tactics development, Saville ordered the establishment of the Air Defense Operational Training Unit. Its formation was ordered by the Third Air Force on Mar. 26, 1942; four days later its name was changed to the Interceptor Command School. This new entity was commanded by Col. Willis R. Taylor.

Training Begins

One of the units assigned to the school was the 50th Pursuit Group (Interceptor). The 50th Group (along with its 10th, 81st and 313th Pursuit Squadrons (Interceptor)) moved from Key Field near Meridian, Mississippi, to Orlando Air Base in Florida, where they joined up with other organizations to establish the Interceptor Command School in late March 1942. Colonel Taylor had outlined in his original plan of Mar. 18, 1942, for the Air Defense Operational Training Unit to be made up of a number of sections. Section X was Night Fighter. On June 10, night-fighting enthusiast Maj. Donald B. Brummel was made commanding officer of the 81st Fighter Squadron (Sp). The 81st was given the responsibilities of night fighter operations. With the liquid state of organization, the Night Fighter Department was established and Major Brummel was assigned as its director some ten days later.

One of Brummel's first actions was to interview Capt. Leonard R. Hall. Hall had been assigned to the Interceptor Command School that past May. Because of his background in electronics and seismic exploration work, he was

brought to Brummel's attention. The interview apparently went well, because Hall was assigned as the assistant director and officer in charge of tactics and techniques. Captain Hall would soon be the first radar observer (R/O) trained in the AAF.

The British were far advanced compared to the United States in night fighting, pushed to this position by the realities of war. Brummel and Hall were soon on their way to England to observe RAF night fighter squadrons in action, and to arrange for the transfer of some British Mark IV AI radar equipment to the fledgling night fighter organization at Orlando.

The XP-61 made its maiden flight in late May 1943. Not long after, Brummel and Hall were on their way to southern California to visit the Northrop plant. While there they were checked out in the XP-61 by Northrup test pilot John Myers. Myers would check out many AAF pilots in the combat theaters some two years later. By the end of July more reorganization took place, and the Night Fighter Department became the Night Fighter Division of the Fighter Department. All the while plans were being redrawn, and an acute shortage of men and equipment persisted.

In July, the 81st Fighter Squadron (Sp) received one B-18 Bolo and a number of P-70s, with which they were to start night fighter training.

By the end of September the Night Fighter Department (Dark) was activated and the 81st Fighter Squadron (Sp) was detached from the 50th Fighter Group (Sp) and placed directly under the Department for training and operations. Training had picked up; Class

'42-A with twenty pilots and twenty observers started training at the beginning of the month. The flying would be accomplished in three T-50s, three DB-7s and twenty-three P-70s.

In early October a metamorphosis of the 81st Fighter Squadron occurred in which the 348th and 349th Night Fighter Squadrons were formed. The 81st was stripped of almost all men and equipment. Maj. Griffin D. Davis, commanding officer of the 81st, took over the 348th in mid-October; he was also responsible for the attached 349th. The 81st was declared inactive by the first of October. Major Davis reported directly to Donald Brummel, now a Lieutenant Colonel, who headed the Night Fighter Section of the Fighter Command School.

Their immediate requirements were to train key personnel for two squadrons that were destined for Hawaii and one for Panama. Pressure was put on the training squadrons to produce the required key personnel for these three operational squadrons. On October 16 it was agreed between the school and the Directorate of Air Defense that by the end of November they would provide four qualified R/Os, twenty qualified AI mechanics, twenty-four pilots and eighteen observer trainees.

This ambitious training program could not be carried out. Because of the lack of operational training aircraft, spare parts and other flying requirements (target towing, for instance), not even half of the flying training requirements were met. Classes '42-A and B would be graduated in early December with only eighty percent of the planned flight training; training which, because of the lack of proper equipment, was not of high quality. As all this was going on, the AAF School of Applied Tactics (AAFSAT) was activated on November 1. It included the Fighter Command School operations, and expanded its role in a number of areas.

In late December the two night fighter squadrons were switched from the Night Fighter Section of the Fighter Command School back to the 50th Fighter Group (Sp); a move to "increase administration efficiency" according to the 348th NFS history. The Night Fighter Section remained active and was responsible for setting tactical employment and broad training directive for the night fighter squadrons.

Overseas Deployment

In early January 1943, the 349th NFS moved from Orlando Air Base to Kissimmee, Florida. With this, a major shuffle of officers and men between the 348th and 349th night fighter squadrons occurred. Capt. Amberse M. Banks became the first commanding officer of the 349th. Between late January and late February 1943, the 414th, 415th, 416th and 417th night fighter squadrons were activated. A number of the seasoned personnel from the 348th and 349th transferred into these four operational squadrons. Captain Banks, newly assigned CO of the 349th, became the CO of the 415th. All four of these operational squadrons would be sent to England to receive training in British Beaufighter night fighters after their short stay in Florida.

The 414th and 415th NFSs received only about two months of training in Florida. Their ground echelons received additional training before joining the air echelons in North Africa in early July. The 416th and 417th NFSs arrived in England in mid-May as complete squadrons for their RAF-sponsored training.

In mid-March 1943, Lt. Col. Brummel, the driving force behind the night fighter program at Orlando, transferred to the Aircraft Equipment Board of AAFSAT. Replacing him was Lt. Col. Winston W. "Winkie" Kratz, who had just arrived from a tour of duty in England. He had been assistant operations officer for VIII Fighter Command and as Eighth Air Force headquarters liaison officer. As the latter, he served as liaison officer with the planning group under Sir Sholto Douglas, then RAF fighter commander. The group was drawing the initial plans for fighter deployment in connection with the Normandy invasion. Kratz was befriended by Air Vice Marshal Mac Gregor during his tour. Through this connection, he was able to fly with the RAF's 605 Squadron—a night intruder outfit.

In the midst of activating and training additional night fighter squadrons and pleading for additional aircraft and other scarce equipment, another reorganization was put into motion. The training squadrons, along with the embryonic 418th and 419th night fighter squadrons, were removed, again, from the 50th Fighter Group's command and assigned to the Night Fighter Division of

AAFSAT's Air Defense Department on April Fools' Day. The Night Fighter Division was a new division of the Air Defense Department, succeeding the Night Fighter Section.

The nuclei of the AAF's night fighter training organization in Orlando, Florida, pose in front of one of their P-70As in July 1943. From the left are: Lt. Col. Winston W. Kratz; Capt. Carroll C. Smith (later to become CO of the 418th NFS in the SWPA, and the leading AAF night fighter ace); Flt. Lt. Carol Kutelvasher (Czech night fighter ace of the RAF who had 26 Huns to his credit); Capt. Oris B. Johnson (later to be CO of the Ninth Air Force's 422nd NFS, the AAF's highest scoring NFS); and an unidentified Captain Kratz

Night fighter trainees wear night goggles prior to flying a night training mission. This practice, along with a diet of carrots for better night vision, was left behind when they entered the combat theaters. Odell

The insignia of the 416th NFS.

The insignia of the 420th NFS.

The activation of the 421st NFS on May 1 made them the third tactical night fighter squadron in the night fighter training program. Activity only heightened as orders came down from Washington to activate a squadron a month. The training organization needed to expand! Thus the 420th NFS was activated on June 1 at Kissimmee (it would move to Dunnellon, Florida, on July 19). Commanding the 420th NFS was Maj. William C. Odell. Major Odell had gone to England in 1942 with the 1st Pursuit Squadron (Night Fighter) and had received night fighter training with the RAF. He would later go to the Pacific as CO of the 547th NFS.

Operational Training Group

Now with three training squadrons, the tasks were broken up into three major functions. The 348th NFS at Orlando provided the initial phases, including instrument flying. The 349th NFS at Kissimmee carried out transition training, while at Dunnellon Army Air Field the 420th provided operational training.

July 15, 1943, was a red-letter day for the night fighters. For a long time, efforts had been taken to establish a night fighter organization as a separate group. Back when the 349th Night Fighter Squadron was first activated, it was initially considered a "provisional group." It had finally come to fruition with the activation of the 481st Night Fighter Operational Training Group (NFOTG). The Night Fighter Division was disbanded, and Lt. Col. Winston Kratz, who had been chief of the division, became the 481st NFOTG's commanding officer.

Black Widow Arrives

In mid-September 1943 the plane that they all had been waiting for arrived—the Black Widow. The initial YP-61 they received that day did not have the AI radar installed yet. Eventually the SCR-520, a preproduction version of the SCR-720 that was fitted to the operational P-61s, was installed. Soon, additional YP-61s and a few P-61As were assigned. These aircraft were used in both the night fighter training program and in the flight-test program that the P-61 was entering (including experiments with turret/gun configurations).

Though they probably saw the P-61, the 418th, 419th and 421st night fighter squadrons shipped out to the Southwest Pacific Area (SWPA) between late September and early November 1943 without any training in it. Their first operational aircraft, received in-theater, were the P-70, P-38 and B-25. When they did receive their own P-61s, they had only abbreviated in-field training on how to fly and maintain them, but this was not until well into 1944. The first operational squadron to be trained in the P-61 prior to deployment overseas was the 422nd NFS.

With a number of squadrons already in the combat theaters along with those in the training cycle, and still more scheduled for activation, thought had to be given to training replacement crews for the operational squadrons. To accomplish this the 424th Night Fighter Squadron was activated on Nov. 27, 1943. Under the command of Maj. Hubbard K. Gayle, Jr., the squadron commenced operations at Orlando Air Base, along with the 481st NFOTG and the 348th NFS.

California Operations

Now that the night fighter training was well under way, and they were finally starting to receive the equipment needed to carry out their mission, what would not be expected? A move to California? That is just what happened in January 1944.

The 481st NFOTG and its four night fighter squadrons took up residence up and down central California's San Joaquin Valley. The main base of operations was established at Hammer Field near Fresno. Other airfields and airports used were Salinas, Delano and Bakersfield. In California, the 481st NFOTG came under the control of Fourth Air Force's IV Fighter Command.

The structure of the night fighter training squadrons in California was as follows: the 348th under the command of Lt. Col. Griffith D. Davis provided instrument training; the 349th commanded by Lt. Col. William R. Yancey performed the transition training phase; and Lt. Col. William C. Odell's 420th provided the final phase of operational training. The 424th NFS under Major Gayle still provided replacement training.

Three operational squadrons were in training in Florida when the orders to move came down. The 423rd and 425th

The first P-61 to arrive at Orlando was a YP-61, serial number 41–18887. In this November 1943 photo the YP-61 is piloted by Colonel Kratz as it flies in formation with one of the night fighter training center's P-70 *aircraft flown by Capt. Larry Leith (senior instrument instructor pilot for the training program). The P-70,* Black Magic, *was named after a popular song of the time.* Kratz

A YP-61, Black Widow, *in the skies over Florida. Peter Raymen, who would later be a gunner in the 6th NFS, painted the name on this aircraft shortly after its arrival. Flown quite often by pilots Porter B. Williamson and Larry Leith, it was used for a multitude of purposes. It was a demonstrator to show the brass the capabilities of the P-61, was part of the P-61 evaluation program and was used in training neophyte night fighters.* Kratz

night fighter squadrons moved along with the training organization. The 422nd NFS moved from Kissimmee to Orlando where they continued receiving ground training. The lack of training aircraft stopped the flight training activities—about the best the pilots could do was to get a little flight time in Piper Cubs.

The California night fighter operations had been in operation for just three months when the IV Fighter Command along with the 481st NFOTG, 348th, 349th, 420th and 424th night fighter squadrons were disbanded. In its place, the 319th Wing was established, under the command of Col. Ralph A. Snavely. Lieutenant Colonel Kratz was assigned to the Wing and remained in charge of the night fighter training program. The operational training unit (OTU) duties were assigned to the 450th Army Air Forces Base Unit (AAFBU).

Black Maria *reveals her radar antenna through a clear plexiglass radome. Note also the high visibility afforded the crew by the greenhouse design of the crew nacelle. The YP-61 was both evaluated and used in the* training environment by the USAAF night-fighting organization. The exact purpose of the clear radome is unknown. *Bowers/Castle Graphics*

This YP-61-NO, serial number 41-18882, like the XP-61-NO had the smooth canopy and flat-black paint. The artwork on the nose was applied to this aircraft when it was used in a training film.

The 450th was made up of a number of lettered squadrons (for example, A, B, C, T-1, T-2 and so on) which were expressed as 450th AAFBU (A Sq). Replacement training unit duties were assigned to the 451st AAFBU which had a squadron structure similar to the 450th. These units operated at the previous fields used by the 481st NFOTG in the San Joaquin Valley. The 441st AAFBU provided gunnery training out of Van Nuys in the San Fernando Valley area of southern California and the 403rd AAFBU at Hammer Field provided other night fighter training required in support of the 319th Wing.

The last operational squadron to be trained by the 481st NFOTG was the 423rd NFS. The squadron left Bakersfield less than a week prior to the group being disbanded. The 423rd NFS arrived in England in mid-March 1944. An interesting thing happened to this squadron. Before they received their P-61s, headquarters decided that they could be better utilized as a night photographic squadron. The squadron designation was changed to 155th Photographic Squadron in late June and they were supplied with A-20Js. They performed their new mission admirably.

On to the Pacific

Starting with the 426th NFS, activated on New Year's Day of 1944, a total of six operational squadrons were formed and trained in California. The last of the string was the 550th NFS, activated on June 1, 1944. The squadron's training was completed on August 25. They left beautiful Visalia, California, for a sojourn to the Pacific, with a short intermission in Hawaii, where the battle-tested 6th NFS took them under their wing.

A good number of the experienced personnel who had been in the training

A P-61A-10 assigned to stateside training duties. Typical for the P-61s used in the training squadrons was the serial number being painted on the lower surfaces of both wings (easy to identify those hot pilots who liked to buzz), and the last two digits of the serial painted on the vertical stabilizer. Smithsonian

squadrons transferred into the last four operational squadrons formed. With the departure of the last operational squadron, the training of replacement crews continued until war's end. As in Florida, new and modified equipment was always being tried. The use of the P-38 as a night fighter using locally modified P-38s carrying radar was tried out. When the P-38M night fighter Lightnings were received from Lockheed, squadrons were formed to train crews for the Pacific war. Only four of these

aircraft got in-theater. They were integrated into the P-61-equipped 418th and 421st night fighter squadrons for a while during the immediate postwar period.

Night fighter training, as was the realm of night fighting, was a pioneering effort. They accomplished what they did because of the courage and farsightedness of the few in this new field of combat. The lack of equipment and support hindered but did not deter them.

Chapter 5

Nipponese Widow-maker

By mid-1944, American forces had been waging war in the Pacific for two and a half years. It had been a hard struggle, one that would go on for some time to come. One of the Army Air Forces units that had been embroiled in this conflict from the beginning was the 6th Pursuit (later Night Fighter) Squadron. This is a proud unit, one that can trace its lineage back to 1917. But on December 7 in 1941, it was decimated by the Japanese navy's attack on the Hawaiian Islands.

The 6th's entire fleet of recently received P-40Bs was turned to a pile of scrap. Pulling together what remained of its fighter force, the 18th Pursuit Group (which the 6th Pursuit Squadron was part of) became operational again, though they were quite under strength, flying P-36s and P-40s. With jittery nerves and numerous reports of Japanese night air attacks and invasions, a night fighter defense force was established by the 18th Group. The theory was that each of its squadrons would provide two pilots and aircraft nightly, on a rotating basis, to provide night cover for the Islands.

As what happens with so many "good ideas," it didn't work out. Conflicts of schedules, limited aircraft availability, interference with day operations all spelled failure. So the task of providing night protection fell to one unit—the 6th Pursuit Squadron. Even with this new assignment, they still were required to perform day operations. This dual role of day/night fighter operations would be the 6th's plight through 1944.

The night fighter operations of the 6th Pursuit Squadron were bolstered with the receipt of its first night fighter aircraft in September 1942. The first of about twenty-four dull-black P-70s came to rest in its nest. This didn't bring cheers from the pilots, however. This twin-engined "bomber" was not what the hot-shot fighter jock wanted to zoom around in. Confusion reigned would be an understatement. What was a night fighter? What was he supposed to do? Answers to these questions were not soon coming. Better yet, who was going to operate the radar? The T.O. (Technical Order, an official document that tells how to operate or maintain a piece of equipment) called for an R/O (radar operation), but the 6th didn't have any, much less know what one was.

These, and many more problems, were worked out in 1942 and 1943. The 6th, redesignated a night fighter squadron in early 1943, met the challenges and did well with what they had. It

Fresh off their seagoing transport, P-61s move up the dock on Guadalcanal. The P-61s were a welcome sight to the 419th NFS which *had been flying P-38 day fighters and P-70s in defense of Guadalcanal and the surrounding islands in the Solomons. USAF*

seems fitting that this unit, the first operational AAF night fighter squadron, would be the first to reequip with the P-61 Black Widow. In about April 1944 the Widows started arriving at the Hawaiian Air Depot where their protective cosmolene covering was removed and wing outer panels were attached. When the first olive-drab-over-gray Widows were turned over to the fighting 6th, Northrop test pilot John Myers was on hand to demonstrate the big bird's qualities and check out the flight crews.

The Widow Arrives

On Guadalcanal in the central Pacific, the 419th NFS was next to turn in their much-to-be-desired P-70s and P-38s for their new mount. As Japanese operations were winding down in this area, it was the perfect time for the conversion to take place. The 419th's Detachment A was recalled from Bougainville (in the Solomon Islands) toward the end of the month, and a big push was put on to make the squadron combat ready and move to an area where their services were dearly needed.

Based at Nadzab, New Guinea, the Fifth Air Force's 421st NFS started sending crews to Brisbane, Australia, in late May to check out in their new aircraft. Upon their arrival, Northrop test pilot

The 419th NFS's CO, Maj. Emerson Y. Baker, axis toward the Guadalcanal runway shortly after the Widow's arrival. Northrop ent test pilot John Myers and tech rep M.

Scott Johnson to the Pacific to help transition the night fighters in the combat areas into the P-61. USAF

John Myers and tech rep M. Scott Johnson found that some of the Brisbane P-61s had been assembled and flown, all this without factory assistance and almost no technical information. Myers later stated: "It is forever to the credit of the men of the service squadrons that they had both the will and the ingenuity to do this. And it's just as much to the credit of the boys who got in and flew the ships without even a pilot's instruction book. Naturally, there were some misunderstandings all around, and in most cases, they weren't able to get the most out of the ship. It didn't take us long to iron out these minor difficulties, and then the boys went for the Widow in a big way."

Saipan Area

The next advance by the Allied forces in the Pacific was to the Marianas, east of the Philippines. Its strategic importance was to serve as a forward base for the AAF's long-range B-29s. Bases were to be established on the

After checking out the 419th NFS on Guadalcanal, Northrop's John Myers and M. Scott Johnson went down to New Guinea in the Southwest Pacific Area, where they repeated the transformation with the battle-tested 418th and 421st NFSs. These units were not remorseful at all in trading in their B-25Hs, P-70s and P-38s for their new mount. Escort Widow that accompanied Northrop's Myers and Charles A. Lindbergh to Mt. Hagen required RNP (real native power) to pull it from the New Guinea mud. Wolford

A detachment of the 6th NFS stop over at Kwajalein Atoll on their way to Saipan Island in the Marianas in the summer of 1944. Installed in the dorsal turret cavity in place of their standard armament are long-range ferry tanks which enabled them to cross the many miles of Pacific Ocean. USAF

islands of Saipan, Tinian and Guam, from which waves of Superfortresses would strike at the home islands of the Japanese empire. To protect these B-29s during the hours of darkness, Hawaii's 6th Night Fighter Squadron sent out a detachment under the command of Maj. George W. Mulholland.

Six P-61s, aircrews and support personnel were dispatched to Saipan. Along with the first waves of Marines to land on Saipan in June 1944 was Lt. John G. Pabst, a fighter director of the 6th NFS. He had their first mobile Ground Control Intercept (GCI) station set up and ready to operate soon afterward. The 6th NFS Widows arrived at Isely Field on Saipan on June 21, and their first mission was flown on the twenty-fourth. First blood for the Widow in any theater was drawn on the night of June 30, 1944. Second Lt. Dale F. Haberman was flying with his regular R/O, Flight Officer (F/O) Raymond P. Mooney that evening. Haberman recalled:

"We were vectored on the bogie at 7,000 ft. with Mooney insisting that we had two targets in formation on our scope. We chased them from 7,000 to 23,000 ft. over a 25 minute period and never did get quite to their altitude. I also forgot the radio and left it on transmit so the whole intercept was heard over the entire Saipan area.

"Admiral Hoover allegedly enjoyed the mission pilot/R/O conversation immensely. At any rate, I finally got a visual on the bogie, a Betty with a Zero on her right wing turning toward the island, up much higher than we were. I pulled the Widow up on her tail and nailed the Betty in the port engine, while the Zero flipped over and came down on our rear with us in a full stall, high blower, engines at 300 degrees C and throttles over the stops.

"We wound up going straight down, Mooney looking up the Zero's gun barrels telling me to twist port or starboard to make the Zero's gunfire miss. We left him like he was in reverse. He also disappeared from the Condor base scope so we don't know what happened. I saw the Betty finally explode near the island, also witnessed by the entire area and suddenly realized we were buffeting badly and were way over the redline. In those days we called it compressibility. I pulled her out at 1,500 ft. and since nothing seemed bent or broken we

Moonhappy, *named for its pilot Dale "Hap" Haberman and R/O Ray Mooney, was assigned to the 6th NFS. This artwork is a* later version showing a lady laying in a crescent moon with stars in her hair and on her shoes. Kenn Rust

The earlier version of Moonhappy *showing two men (one armed with a club) riding an angry moon. Lieutenant Haberman, right, is credited with four Bettys. Ray Mooney, his* R/O, in on the left. On June 30, 1944, Haberman and Mooney scored the first aerial victory for the Black Widow. E. Thomas

landed. Subsequent inspection found nothing wrong and a report was submitted to Northrop."

A week later, a P-61 piloted by 1st Lt. Francis C. Eaton, with 2nd Lt. James E. Ketchum (R/O) and S. Sgt. W. S. Anderson (observer-gunner) took off to relieve the swing shift. They weren't airborne more than a few minutes when ground control radioed them that a bogey had been detected; "Bluegrass 53" (code name for Eaton's crew) was vectored 120 degrees. This maneuver brought them too close to slightly trigger-happy "friendly" surface vessels. Anti-aircraft fire from the ships was too close for comfort, which forced Eaton to put his aircraft in a sharp diving, banking turn. Again ground control called, "Vector 040, bogey at 8,000 ft. altitude." Now, Eaton had to gain altitude. "Vector 360 degrees." The incoming enemy bomber was only four miles from the Widow. "Vector 120 degrees." Now, Ketchum had a blip on his scope—the enemy. Tensely, Anderson was straining his eyes

trying to make a visual contact with the bomber somewhere in the endless darkness.

The distance was closing. Eaton's mind was working: "Have to drop flaps, don't want to overshoot. Too fast, too fast, have to S-turn." "Two miles to target," Ketchum called out over the intercom; 600 ft. "There he is," Ketchum said. Slightly to port and at the same altitude was a Japanese Betty. No results were seen from the Widow's first barrage of gunfire. The Betty started turning to the left and more lethal lead was spewn by the P-61. Direct hit in the left wing. Closer, closer, closer. Eaton now had his black beast dead astern of the Betty. The Widow shuddered with the roar of cannon and machine-gun fire. Scratch another Betty!

It wasn't long afterward that a SWPA (Southwest Pacific Area) Widow of the 421st showed what the venomous sting of the Black Widow could do. On the night of July 7, 1944, 1st Lt. Owen M. Wolf and his crew, 2nd Lt. Byron N.

Allain (R/O) and S. Sgt. Donald H. Trabing (gunner) were among the crews standing alert duty. Their official report reads as follows:

"Scrambled by Fighter Sector, I took off immediately after sounding of red alert and stayed at a minimum altitude on a course Southwest from Owi Strip and to avoid friendly A/A (anti-aircraft). I climbed rapidly to 10,000 ft. on a SSW heading. GCI called in a vector, and I proceeded on this course, but bad weather obscured the radar scope so that no contact was made.

"Next I was vectored on a course parallel to and ahead of the bogie. At the direction of the radar observer (Allain) I throttled back, turning slightly port so that the enemy plane, if it continued on its course, would cross in front of the nose of my plane. By this time my plane was out of the range of the GCI Controller, but I requested and received permission to continue the search visually and through my own radar equipment.

"On a general westerly heading I searched the area for about five minutes, slight rain hampering the sighting. GCI ordered me to return then if I had no contact. I asked for a few minutes more and received permission. Suddenly a blip appeared on the radar scope at 0055/K, and the radar observer took control of the course of the *Queen*. He directed the ship on a gentle turn to the port and then to the starboard bringing my plane directly behind and below the tail of the enemy plane. At that time we were one mile behind the bogie at 6,500 ft.

"Throttling back at the direction of the radar observer so that we would not overshoot, I closed quickly on the enemy plane. The plane was a twin-engine bomber with tapered wings and a thin fuselage, apparently a Sally or a Dinah. The exhaust pattern, bright orange, was distinct and visible. It extended below each nacelle at an angle of 45 degrees to the rear and 65 degrees in width as viewed from behind.

"Upon obtaining a visual on the plane, I throttled slightly forward and opened fire with all eight guns. At a range of 150 yards the first burst scored a direct hit on the starboard engine of the Japanese plane. The engine flamed and part of the fuselage exploded, throwing fragments into the path of my ship

Husslin' Hussy, *a glossy-black P-61 belonging to the 6th NFS. The 6th was assigned to the Seventh Air Force and was the first of the* operational squadrons to receive the P-61. Kenn Rust

and slightly damaging the underside of my fuselage and the port spinner. I continued to press the attack, firing long bursts.

"I could see the 20 mm exploding against the enemy plane, and the tracers of the 50 cal. entering its outline. The aircraft suddenly flamed and fell off into a steep dive. I followed directly on its tail, continuing to fire, until my indicated air speed reached more than 500 mph.

"The enemy plane crashed in the water along the beach on the Southwest of Japen Island [also known as Yapen]. It exploded when it hit the water, and I could see both the engines thrown to the shore. There was no return fire from the enemy plane as it was apparently unaware of my presence until the attack. None of the enemy aircrew were seen to parachute."

The Seventh Air Force's only night fighter squadron, the 6th, remained split during the last half of 1944, headquarters being in Hawaii. Detachment A's primary mission was the protection of the B–29's station at West Field on Saipan. The night fighters flew CAP (combat air patrol) and interception-alert-type missions and aided in the rescue of many crippled and lost B–29s on the

This Sleepy Time Gal *appears to be the same aircraft as* Sleepy Time Gal II, *as there is a* remnant of the old name still visible. Kenn Rust

Named after a popular song of the day, many night fighter squadrons had a Sleepy Time Gal, *this being the 6th NFS's* Sleepy Time Gal II. *Pilot Capt. Ernest Thomas and R/O Lt. John Acre have two confirmed victories, one each in the Saipan and Iwo Jima areas of the central Pacific.* Haberman

Nightie Mission, *a P–61 belonging to the 6th NFS. The light shining through the frosted* radome reveals the radar antenna. Kenn Rust

51

way back from raids on Japan. Though the .50 caliber gun turrets in the six Black Widows of the 6th Night Fighter Squadron were in a locked forward firing position (these were actually four .50 caliber machine guns secured in the upper portion of the turret cavity sans turret mechanism and covered by a nonstandard turret cover; it is uncertain if this modification was made only in the field or if some or all were made at the Hawaiian Air Depot) and fired only by the pilot, a gunner was still carried on many missions as an extra pair of eyes to ensure the proper identification of enemy aircraft prior to attack. By the end of the year, the 6th NFS had no fewer than a half-dozen kills with only two losses, neither of which were due to enemy action.

As the Allied forces advanced in the central Pacific, more bases needed night protection. Seventh Air Force night fighter strength was bolstered in the latter half of 1944 by the 548th NFS under the command of Maj. Robert D. Curtis, arriving in Hawaii in mid-September, followed by the 549th a month later which was commanded by Maj. Joseph E. Payne. These new squadrons remained in Hawaii through the remainder of the year, gaining experience under the tutelage of the seasoned 6th NFS. One detachment of the 548th under Capt. William Dames flew to Saipan in December to bolster the 6th's detachment there.

Noemfoor Island Area

Southwest Pacific Area forces were on the move during mid-1944 also. Heavy bombers were using Hollandia, New Guinea, as an advance base. Wakde, Biak, Owi and Woleai in the Schouten Islands off the northern coast of New Guinea fell to Allied forces in rapid succession, and by June 2 the invasion of Noemfoor Island (in the Netherland East Indies) was in progress. Here, operations began shortly afterward, and the night skies of Noemfoor would have to be protected from Japanese air strikes. Detachment A of the 419th was transferred from Nadzab to Noemfoor in late July. By the fifth of August the 419th Night Fighter Squadron had their first victory claim. Capt. Al Lukas, commanding the detachment, made a perfect intercept on a Japanese Sally bomber and destroyed it with great ease.

The 418th NFS arrived at Morotai, Indonesia, to take part in operations against Japanese in the southern Philippines. The air echelon of the 418th moved to Owi Island in mid-September to aid the 421st NFS. During their three-week stay on the island, the 418th continued their training patrols and alternated every other night for the island's defense with the 421st NFS.

The 547th, under the command of Col. William C. Odell, joined the Fifth Air Force in late September. They would end the war with a relatively low number of kills. Their greatest contributions would lie in the pioneering night fighter

One of the 419th's P-61s in the vicinity of Noemfoor Island in the Netherland East Indies. The placement of squadron aircraft numbers near the nose of the aircraft was unique to the 419th. National Archives

work they would soon undertake. The 547th was made up of many pilots and R/Os who had night fighter and night intruder experience with the Royal Canadian Air Force, RAF and the US Eighth and Twelfth air forces. Many of them were well known to the commanding generals in the area.

Soon after the 547th joined Fifth Air Force, Brig. Gen. Paul B. Wurtsmith, commanding general of V Fighter Command, had a meeting with Colonel Odell. Odell later said:

"Aside from operating as a night fighter unit with the ordinary missions most performed, the 547th was used to back up and reinforce many night fighter efforts in the area. This was determined by General Wurtsmith at the time the 547th arrived in the theater. His decision was based on the need for experienced and combat-knowledgeable crews, and the 547th had many such crews. Whenever a lesser trained night fighter unit required assistance or were unable to perform adequately, the 547th was called upon to step in and give the extra effort needed.

"At a meeting at Owi Island in General Wurtsmith's quarters, this was explained to me during mid-September of 1944. Gen. Earl W. Barnes, who commanded XIII Fighter Command, had made this proposal to General Wurtsmith because of his first-hand knowledge of the capabilities of the crews of the 547th. This proposal was made by General Barnes with foresight since the 547th also gained the commitment of being on call by General Barnes whenever the Thirteenth Air Force also needed the help of well trained crews. Thus the 547th had the opportunity to take part in operations at the most crucial times and in a great many places. It also accounts for the use of the 547th to test advanced equipment such as the P-38s with APS-4 Radar."

Morotai Area

The 418th's air echelon arrived at Morotai on Oct. 5, 1944. Very little occurred during the first couple of nights because of bad weather. On the third night they experienced their first red alert and their first victory with the P-61. Two crews of the 418th were on airborne patrol at the time of the alert. One of the crews was the commanding officer, Maj. Carroll C. Smith, and his

R/O, Lt. Phil Porter. The incoming Japanese were closer to Smith than to the other crew; subsequently, Smith was vectored by GCI to an intercept course where a quick radar intercept was completed. This is what took place, according to Smith:

"That Jap pilot tooling his twin-engine Dinah Mark II toward our airstrip at Morotai wasn't worried. At 8,000 ft. his fighter was invisible, he thought, his 20 mm cannon and 7.7 mm machine guns would protect him in a clinch, and as a last resort he could climb a mile in 90 seconds or so to evade us.

"He hadn't the foggiest notion that Lt. Phil Porter and I were floating in the moonlight over the field, throttled to minimum cruising speed; we were saving gas to make sure we had plenty in case a Nip came over.

"He still wasn't worried when our ground control picked him up and flashed the first order: 'Darkie 1 from Nightie. Climb to 8,000 . . . cruise two zero zero . . . range about 12 miles.' Instantly I turned my attention to my instruments. Phil shouted instructions as I swung the Black Widow into the new heading. I flipped on the water injection to pull another 6 inches of manifold pressure. That meant 200 to 300 more horsepower from the big Pratt & Whitneys . . . 300 feet per minute faster climb.

"While ground control continued directing us toward the incoming fighter, I climbed and turned with everything jammed to the firewall. The Jap had headed for our field, bearing a load of medium bombs. A few more seconds and we spotted each other in the brilliant moonlight, at a range of 2,000 feet. He then was within a mile of our base.

"Talking about evasive action! That boy could really fly; he was worried now, for the Nips had heard about these deadly Black Widows. Ours was fairly

The insignia of the 418th NFS.

The Virgin Widow, *a P–61 belonging to the 6th NFS. Note the word virgin has two lines marked through it. These lines were drawn* after the Virgin *made her first kill.* Alyn T. Lloyd

new, but those four 20 mm cannons spouting flame and shells from the belly spelled certain and swift destruction to any fighter and bomber within range.

"I could see him easily as he climbed. His maneuver was no good, for the Widow was climbing even faster. I began overhauling him at 17,500 ft. Three bursts failed to hit. The fourth and fifth seemed to do little damage. For the sixth I managed to pull within 150 ft. of his left wing and cut loose with a full deflection shot as he roared past. Chunks exploded from the glistening Dinah. He fell, burning, a plume of smoke falling into the earth."

Tacloban

With the invasion of Leyte (an island in the Philippines) the 421st left the 547th in defense of the Owi area. The first Army Air Force units to land on Leyte included the 421st's ground contingent. The air echelon caught up with the ground personnel ten days later at their base at Tacloban, on Leyte. The Japanese helped in celebrating the Americans' arrival with an average of eighteen nightly raids, a record thirty-nine raids occurring in one twenty-four-hour period.

Between the enemy action, mud and poor facilities the 421st was more of

A close-up view of the P-61A-1-NO Skippy shows a Japanese flag denoting a victory for its pilot, Lt. Dave T. Corts of the 421st NFS.

Note the checkered spinner. Tacloban, Leyte Island, Nov. 2, 1944. US Army

a liability than an asset their first few days. On one night patrol a 421st Widow in pursuit of an enemy aircraft was fired upon by friendly ack-ack, while a Japanese aircraft showing its navigation lights was allowed to fly over the field without a shot being fired. Higher headquarters had little understanding of the role that the night fighters should play, and even less sympathy for the 421st, so it delegated them to dawn and dusk patrols in cooperation with Navy PT boats.

This required the Black Widows to fly and fight during daytime hours, not the most suitable conditions for this aircraft. One incident in late November of 1944 turned out to have been a good one for the 421st. D flight was on patrol that evening, under the command of Lt. Owen M. Wolf, when it encountered a formation of seven enemy aircraft: six Zekes and a Hamp—poor old D flight had but four P-61s.

Lieutenant Wolf, with Lt. Byron N. Allain, R/O, and S. Sgt. Emil K. Weishar manning the four .50 calibers in the Widow's turret closed in on one of the Zekes and the Hamp. With the burst from his 20 mm cannons, Wolf sent the Zeke to its destruction. At the same time Weishar, using a deflection shot, sent a volley of fire from his .50s into the cockpit of the Hamp, which blew up and crashed in flames. A third enemy was destroyed expeditiously by Lt. Robert C. Pew's gunner, S. Sgt. Ralph H. McDaniel, who was controlling their turret. Then, possibly mistaking the Widow for a P-38, one of the remaining Zekes that had been orbiting attacked Lt. Hoke Smith's aircraft from the rear. As the Zeke opened fire, Lt. Robert H. Bremer, Smith's R/O, took control of the Widow's turret from Sgt. James W. Pilling and sent a steady burst directly to the rear, shattering the attacking Zeke. When this evening encounter ended, both the 421st and the Japanese aircrews could attest to the value of the four .50 caliber guns in the Widow's lethal turret.

Though the 421st started out with a full complement of aircraft, the heavy nightly attacks of the Japanese, and the daylight fighting that they were forced into, were taking a heavy toll of the 421st's aircraft. Aggravating the situation was the fact that very few spare engines were available in the Southwest Pacific Area. Engines had been dis-

patched to the theater, but most of them were lost due to the fact that the depots at Finschhafen (New Guinea) and Biak (Schouten Islands) failed to "pickle" them when they arrived and prior to their being stored. This failure resulted in the loss of over 400 engines to corrosion. With all these negative factors, the 421st found themselves operating with a total of six aircraft at times.

The inconveniences and "minor" agitations of the Pacific didn't deter the hearty bunch of the 421st, however. One early November morning in 1944, Lt. Albert W. Lockhart and his crew, Lt. Stewart A. Thornton, R/O, and S. Sgt. Joseph Mazur, gunner, were returning from one of their PT coop patrols. The morning rays of the sun were beginning to appear when Lieutenant Lockhart, flying at 7,000 ft. sited two Japanese Tonys flying at about 100 ft. off the deck. Following instructions from higher headquarters for P-61s not to engage the enemy during daylight hours, he radioed in his siting and requested that day fighters be sent up to intercept the incoming enemy. He was asked to repeat his message, and Lockhart did it obligingly. Being asked to repeat it a second time because his transmission was cut off by another aircraft, Lockhart shouted, "Goddamnit! I'll get the bastards myself!" Upon making his intercept, he found that his 50 caliber machine guns in his turret had jammed, but his remaining four 20 mm cannons were more than enough to destroy both of the enemy.

Under the command of Capt. Paul H. Baldwin, a special detachment of the 547th Night Fighter Squadron arrived at Tacloban and took up joint tenancy with the already encamped 421st. Captain Baldwin, the chief R/O of the 547th, arrived with five special aircraft: two P-38s, two P-61s and a B-25. These were far from the standard aircraft configuration. The two P-38s and the B-25 had been modified at Townsville, Australia, to carry APS-4 radar; the modification was performed under the supervision of Western Electric. Both P-38s, remaining one-man aircraft, were equipped with the new radar and painted in the night fighter glossy black paint scheme. The B-25 which was to be used as a training aircraft was equipped with an APS-4 set with three to four scopes for training R/Os or pilots. The 547th obtained P-38

bomb shackles and equipped their special long-range P-61s with external fuel tanks. This special unit arrived at Tacloban on Nov. 9, 1944, and immediately set up operations. This P-38 radar experiment was part of an Air Force project which started sometime earlier at Hammer Field, California. The 547th was chosen to test this equipment under actual combat conditions. The purpose of the P-38 radar experimentation by the 547th was to determine the feasibility of going ahead with production aircraft or cancel the entire project. The crews had received some training in Australia and back on Owi where the 547th was stationed.

Dawn and Dusk Intruder Missions

After their training period, tactical missions of intruding were carried out against isolated Japanese installations in the Dutch East Indies. More tests had been planned from their Owi base, but higher headquarters was very interested in this program and sent the special project to Leyte. Here, dawn and dusk intruder missions were flown over Japanese airdromes in the areas of Sebu,

This artwork adorned the P-61 piloted by Capt. W. T. Bradley, CO of the 421st NFS. Bill Bradley

Negros and lower Luzon, which were 100 to 150 miles from their base. The purpose of these missions was to eliminate or curtail the damaging dawn and dusk missions that the Japanese were flying over Allied installations. It became apparent that this system worked most effectively during the early morning hours.

Japanese fields were seldom illuminated, except when preparations were under way for an upcoming bombing mission. An Allied intruder in the vicinity of Japanese facilities put the station on red alert, and they would not permit their aircraft to take off. To take advantage of the Japanese reaction, a night fighter would remain in the area of an enemy field until it was ascertained that daylight would meet the incoming enemy if a takeoff was ordered. This would place the bombers at the mercy of Allied day fighters. When it was deemed that the hour was past for the initiation of an enemy raid, the intruder would fly to airdromes closer to his own base and repeat this procedure. Because of the speed of the P-38, this maneuver was accomplished with ease, enabling the crew to arrive over the airdrome well in time to cause a red alert before the bombers were allowed to take off.

The results of these missions were easily determined and significant, since no morning or dusk raids were made on Tacloban during the evenings or mornings when the P-38s flew. The nights when they did not fly, the Japanese raided the area. The concept of this entire system was the brain child of the unit's chief R/O, Capt. Paul H. Baldwin.

During their two months operation at Tacloban, the 547th almost lost a Widow when it nearly had its tail shot off by "friendly" antiaircraft (AA). The night fighters often attacked without their IFF (identification, friend or foe) transmitting because the Japanese were able to home and detect aircraft on their own IFF interrogators. As Capt. William Sellers, operations officer of the 547th,

Nocturnal Nemesis, a P-61 of the 421st, is getting a thorough going over between missions. Note the entrance doors and ladder are down. The crew chief is in the pilot's seat checking out the engines. The inset shows the Nemesis's olive-drab-over-gray paint scheme.

was attempting to intercept an enemy aircraft, friendly fire hit the tail section of his Black Widow. Sellers was able to bring in his aircraft successfully, however. At this time, Tacloban's antiaircraft control was regarded as inept by the night fighters. By coincidence, the erring AA battery commander suffered minor abrasions and cuts shortly afterward from an unknown assailant.

The night fighters seemed to have more problems with friendly antiaircraft units than with the enemy during their early operations in the Pacific theater. Soon after their arrival, the 418th Night Fighter Squadron was informed by an antiaircraft colonel that, "Under no circumstances will we hold the ack-ack. This is war, and a night fighter will just have to take his chances." Well, one day while Maj. Carroll C. Smith, commanding officer of the 418th, was flying over the colonel's area during an intercept mission he was fired on by the 90 mm guns of the AA boys. Major Smith's training in target towing prior to becoming a night fighter caused him to not be overly concerned at first. He even went so far as to inform the AA unit by radio how far they were missing him, and helped them calibrate their fire. The fifth salvo almost got him, which brought things to a head with the AA crews. Smith later said: ". . . immediate showdown was had with the anti-aircraft people with much hair pulling and a

casting of doubts upon the ancestry of various and sundry individuals of the coastal artillery." After this, no further troubles along these lines occurred.

Mindoro Area

The 418th was transferred from Morotai to San Jose on Mindoro in late December 1944. In their place the newly arrived 419th NFS took on the duties of area defense. It wasn't smooth sailing for the 418th on its sojourn, though, as the ship carrying most of the ground service equipment was hit by a Kamakazi and sunk. To aid the 418th with its loss of equipment, the air echelon of the 547th, minus its special detachment at Tacloban, was sent to San Jose.

By mid-January the special detachment of the 547th had wrapped up its operation in Tacloban and joined the rest of its unit at San Jose. From there, nearly three months of additional experimentation was carried out. They found that external tanks and bomb shackles attached to the P-61 made it a good long-range night fighter. Also, with the ease of modifying a B-25 to carry APS-4 radar, they felt that the B-25 would make a very effective night intruder. But the P-38 was a different story. The men of the 547th NFS felt it was not at all suitable for night fighting and was possibly more tactically suitable for dawn and dusk patrols, where fighting would probably occur during

daylight hours. It was also considered tactically suitable for intruding in areas that had distinct topographical features. This, however, would necessitate more training in intruder navigation for the pilots.

The 418th Night Fighter Squadron's Major Smith also tried using the P-38 as a night fighter. They went one step further, devising a two-place P-38 conversion. Smith reported:

"We had a little radar observer named of Dubasik who wrote the report on it. He weighed 110 lb. and was about 5 ft. 2 in. He wrote that there's no problem of space for the radar observer, but he failed to point out his own dimensions. We put the old 540 radar, out of the P-70s, into some P-38s. It worked moderately well, though we didn't do too much good with them. Then later on in the States they made the M model. That was sort of the same idea, but ours was just strictly a little local unit modification of putting in a jumpseat for a radar observer to use and installing a 540 radar which came out of a P-70."

Swapping Widows for Hellcats

Much has been made in the past of the swapping of a Marine night fighter squadron for one of the AAF's. The reasons for swapping Marine night fighter squadron VMF(N)-541 stationed on Peleliu Island in the Palau Group for the 421st Night Fighter Squadron (AAF) at

P-61A-10 Snuggle Bunny parked in a line with other members of the 547th NFS on Lin- *gayen airstrip, Luzon, Philippine Islands, 1945.* USAF

Tacloban on Leyte Island seem to be quite muddled. The idea was that the Marine's air echelon was to operate from Tacloban for a period of two weeks being supported by the 421st ground personnel; the 421st air echelon would operate out of Peleliu, there being supported by the Marines.

Conditions at Tacloban were very primitive. The strip was muddy and had practically no operative runway, no taxiways or parking facilities. It was not set up at all as a night fighter airstrip and runway lights were not used for fear of bringing down the wrath of Japanese night intruders. Because of the lack of runway lighting, the P-61 crews found that they had to make up to five passes at times in trying to locate their airfield. Transportation was poor and walks through at least one mile of mud at early morning hours were frequently necessary in order to reach roads going to the fighter strips. With such poor field conditions, aircraft with standard landing

gear such as the F6F-5N Hellcats that the Marines were using would be more desirable than the tricycle-geared P-61s of the AAF. This is somewhat supported in *Far East Air Force History Vol. 1,* which reads: "Because of the slowness of the construction process in Leyte, the 22nd Bomb Group (H), and the 421st Night Fighter Squadron were moved to Palau to operate from facilities constructed by Pacific Ocean Area (POA)." But a message from Gen. Douglas MacArthur to Adm. Chester W. Nimitz concerning this trade states: "Japs operating Oscars as night bombers are too fast for the P-61. In Palau the enemy is employing bombers which P-61's can effectively cope with. Would appreciate your considering a temporary swap of night fighter squadrons—the Marine squadron from Palau could operate from Leyte and P-61's to go to Palau."

This does not seem to be realistic, since the Oscar (Nakajima Ki-43) is nearly 50 mph slower than the P-61A.

MacArthur also felt that he was not receiving the dawn and dusk protection that he should have. Here he was right, as the 421st at times operated with no more than six aircraft. This was due to loss of aircraft during daylight operations that they were forced to perform (a classic problem of day fighter higher command not understanding night fighter tactics). Also, the night attacks that were occurring when they landed at Leyte, and continued afterward, took their toll of aircraft grounded because of a lack of spare parts. This condition was somewhat alleviated by the special detachment of the 547th NFS which arrived shortly after the 421st and remained there during the Marines' stay. The 421st Night Fighter Squadron history states that their P-61s were pulled out due to the requirement for a longer range night fighter to cover amphibious landings in the Philippines.

William T. Bradley, then commanding officer of the 421st, stated: "For the

The Spook, *a P-61 flown by the 548th NFS. It met its demise in a night-landing accident.*

In the darkness it clipped the top of another parked Widow.

second landing in the Philippines we were to provide dusk and dawn coverage of the beach head. Our '61s (which had not been modified for external fuel) could only be over the beach head 20 minutes to an hour. This was not enough time, so command made the decision that they would bring in a Marine night fighter squadron in our place."

It is true that the Grumman F6F Hellcats did have a longer range, but the missions that they flew for most of their time did not require this added range.

Whatever the reasons may have been, most likely somewhat political in nature between the Army and Navy, the Marines arrived on Leyte on Dec. 3, 1944, and operated from Tacloban for a period of five weeks, some three weeks longer than anticipated. During their five weeks on Leyte, the Marines did a commendable job, running up a total of twenty-three confirmed enemy aircraft destroyed. However, it should be noted that the Marines had no true night fighter victory, that is, no radar-assisted intercepts. There was only one momen-

A turret-equipped Widow? No! There were a number of turretless Widows that had a fixed four .50 caliber gun installation added in the Pacific theater. Visually, the giveaway is the straight trailing edge of the installation, as opposed to the rounded aft of the turret cover. USAF

60

tary contact on radar through cloud cover, and then the intercept. All their victories were either on dawn or dusk patrols, which the Hellcat is better suited for than the P-61.

The Widows Return

The qualities of the Hellcat as a night fighter were similar to those of the single-place P- 3s that the 547th NFS evaluated. It was a very capable aircraft for fighting during daylight hours and for dawn and dusk patrols, but during inclement weather and moonless nights, the P-61 was found to be far superior. The major weakness of the P-61 was a lack of range and loiter time, both of which were subsequently improved by the addition of external fuel tanks. This was accomplished by field modifications and later on in Northrop's production lines at Hawthorne, California. On the eleventh of January 1945 the Marines went back to the Palau Group, and the air echelon of the 421st returned to Leyte.

The evening of Dec. 29, 1944, was very fruitful for the night fighter team of Maj. Carroll C. Smith and his R/O Lt. Phil Porter of the 418th NFS. Smith recalled:

"Three of us took off shortly before dusk and flew 50 miles south to cover a convoy of 300 ships.

"Three minutes after the light began to fade I sent my two wing planes back and continued my patrol alone. It was perhaps an hour later when the fighter direction messaged: 'Indications plane coming from southwest—8,000 ft.—12 to 15 miles away.'

"I set a collision course, climbing and hoping to intercept the Jap a safe distance from the convoy. I closed in fast and first saw him two miles away, scudding towards a cloud. Both Phil and I identified him instantly, an Irving, similar to a Nick only slightly larger. A deadly 20 mm stinger in the tail and three 12.7 mm machine guns. Mustn't let him get in the first burst.

"For seven minutes I chased the fellow. He turned in and out of the clouds. Gradually we descended. I hit him with a short burst as he entered one patch of cloud, and got away a second burst, the bullet striking around the wing roots when he came out in a turn. His tail stinger was chattering but not for long. Down he dove, burning and disappeared completely. The Irving was swallowed by

the sea at nine o'clock, straight up. We circled only long enough to confirm the kill."

Confirmation gained and up to altitude again, they were once more on station. With a watchful eye, electronic as well as optical, they flew their protective orbit. Only a few minutes passed when Porter spotted another enemy aircraft. It was coming in toward the convoy from their eleven o'clock position. Both Smith and the enemy aircraft were at the same altitude. Due to the enemy's close proximity to the convoy, Smith had no time to maneuver into a more desirable attack from astern. He pushed the throttles wide open and came in for a head-on attack. He dove in order to cut off the Irving before he could start his bomb run.

From 800 ft. away, Smith let loose a short burst from his 20 mm cannons. He observed hits in the canopy area while others opened up the Irving's fuel tanks. Several pieces flew off the aircraft as the plane tumbled and blazed merrily as it glided into the water. A good night's work was done. With two Irvings to his credit and low on gas, they headed back to refuel, rearm, get a cup of coffee and, if possible, forty winks before they would go on local patrol in the early morning hours.

They had been on station for less than thirty minutes during their second patrol of the night when GCI picked up a contact. Vectoring Smith to the unidentified aircraft, the major was able to identify it as a Rufe, a single-engine float plane of the Japanese Imperial Navy. The Rufe could fly low and slow. Its maneuverings made it difficult for the P-61 to catch. On numerous occasions during their low flying, Smith would have the Rufe in his sights only to have it escape because of its tight and low turns. Finally, by lowering his flaps halfway down and cutting his speed to 120 mph, Smith was able to get careful aim on his prey. Letting loose of a short burst at about 150 ft., the Rufe was destroyed with ease.

Going from slow to fast two hours later, Smith and Porter were vectored by GCI once again to an incoming unidentified aircraft. This time it was a Frank. It was somewhat like a Zeke but much faster. The Frank could hit speeds of about 400 mph and faster, much faster than the P-61. Surprise was the only

advantage that the night fighters had on their side. Smith recalled:

"I began to worry. Three kills already. How many rounds of ammunition had I used? Maybe I had a hundred left, but maybe I had only two or three. I had to get him with the first burst! Phil commenced calling off the ranges. When he hit 150, he peered out ahead. I could see the Frank looming up closer and closer. I closed to 75 ft. At that deadly range I pushed the button. Twenty, thirty, maybe forty tapered steel slugs rammed into the Frank. As he exploded I chopped the throttle, dropping back to avoid most of the debris."

With this four-in-one-night kill, Smith and Porter were the top night fighter team in the southwest Pacific. They were not the only 418th team to be lucky that night, as the team of 2nd Lt. George M. Ellings and his R/O, F/O Milton Burman, successfully intercepted and destroyed another Rufe which brought the squadron total of eight enemy aircraft destroyed in a five-day period.

Night Intruder and Escort Missions

With the ever-decreasing enemy night aircraft activities, night fighter squadrons of the Fifth and Thirteenth air forces turned more and more toward the role of night intruders and flying cooperative missions in support of ground operations. One of these coop-

Most of the night fighter squadrons were involved in night interdiction missions. They modified their aircraft to carry bombs and rockets, such as this 550th NFS P-61. USAF

erative missions was a 547th Night Fighter Squadron cover for the Sixth Army's Ranger Battalion's liberation of the POW camp at Cabanatuan on Luzon Island in the Philippines. Flying top cover for the Rangers on this night was Capt. Kenneth R. Schrieber and his R/O, Lt. Bonnie B. Rucks. Captain Schrieber (now a retired USAF lieutenant colonel) recalls that night:

"We didn't observe any road traffic that night so no shots were fired. We could see the Rangers in the trenches along the road as they proceeded towards the POW camp. There were only a few Japs in the tower protecting the camp. The Rangers wanted to surprise the Jap guards before they could kill any of the POW's."

The raid was successful and 411 American Army prisoners were released from their many years of imprisonment.

To enlarge their scope of operations, the 418th and 547th flew extended missions to Formosa and the Chinese mainland. Some of these missions were to fly protective cover for Army B-24

Midnight Mickey, P-61A, serial number 42-5523, piloted by Lt. Myrle W. McCumber of the 6th NFS. McCumber and his R/O, Daniel Hinz, are credited with two Bettys and a probable in the Iwo Jima area. Kenn Rust

Liberators or Navy PB4Y Privateers. On occasions they flew harassment missions armed with 1,000 lb. bombs, causing little destruction but great confusion to the enemy ground installations on Formosa. These wide-ranging missions are graphically illustrated in a report from the 547th NFS:

"A number of highly successful missions employing the *shadow tactics* devised by Capt. Paul H. Baldwin have been completed. Crews of Navy Privateers have high praise for protection given by our crews throughout the South China Sea patrols. Main disadvantage of this type of night fighter escort mission is a difference in range and endurance between the P-61 and Privateer. Although it is most effective during that part of the mission when the P-61 can tail the Navy patrol aircraft. In the past twenty-two days, fourteen such missions were flown during which there were six enemy encounters. All of which were driven off prior to attack upon the Navy aircraft. No kills were made, although two probably-damaged aircraft were reported.

"Upon completion of the field modifications to P-61 aircraft proposed by Lt. Gillespie in which the central turret will be removed, and B-24 fuselage ferry tanks installed in the cavity, greater range and endurance will result and permit night fighter escort 'on-station' time extended. Navy pilots are requesting the P-61 night trailers directly to the squadron, and it is regretable that other commitments prevent full cooperation.

"They have overcome their concern that the trailing night fighter will mistake the Privateer for an enemy aircraft. This was brought out by a day-light demonstration in which two P-61's and our B-25 Fat-Cat craft were used. Lt. Cmdr. J. B. Wilson participated in the demonstration. He was an observer in the trailing aircraft in which six mock attacks were made upon the second P-61 acting as an attacking enemy. The trail P-61 maintained a six to eight mile interval between itself and the B-25. The attacking P-61 injected itself between the trailer and target at ranges from three to five miles behind the B-25. Upon incident of the intermediate echo between the trailer and the blip representing the B-25, the trailer closed to within firing range before the attacking P-61 could close. This type of tactic, in which the escorting night fighter shad-

ows the aircraft to be protected, is valid as long as the range of the airborne radar, and the shadowing aircraft is greater than that possessed by the enemy. It is interesting to note that night attacks upon Navy Privateers have reduced since the shadow tactics have been employed. The conclusion is the Japanese air defense is reluctant to dispatch fighters against a patrol aircraft that has a shadow aircraft in trail. In two recent missions, the tail warning device on the trail P-61 has been triggered, indicating that Japanese night fighters are being vectored against the escort aircraft rather than the patrol bomber. No encounters resulted from these incidents."

Pacific night fighters flew numerous types of missions. It should be realized that the night fighter was intended to be a defensive weapon, but the realities of war have a way of changing many a good plan. In this theater of operations the USAAF night forces flew more offensive missions. They provided air defense during periods of darkness for their home bases while other members of their units would fly in cooperation with Navy PT boats in coordinated raids, cover for Naval fleets and provide cover during darkness for Allied forces on newly acquired beachheads. In preparation for planned advancement, the night fighters would fly intruder missions in the areas in which the Allies would next move.

Field Modifications

The engineering officer for the 547th NFS, Capt. Dale Strausser, received the Bronze Star for his ingenuity in making the P-61 a more effective combat aircraft. He had the turret removed, and installed an internal fuel tank in the fuselage cavity, extending the P-61's range tremendously. To give the P-61 more of a punch on intruder missions, a P-38 bomb shackle was attached directly under the crew nacelle. Shimming was required on one side to make it level, and a 1,000 lb. bomb was attached. An electrical and mechanical emergency release was installed to take care of three such bombs, one beneath the fuselage and one on each of the outer wing pylons that were modified to carry ordnance. This modification proved so successful that Fifth Air Force headquarters gave support to this project, and an additional five aircraft were so modified by the end of February 1945.

Not only were the means to carry the ordnance developed, but the weapons themselves were also developed by the men of the 547th. A crude napalm device consisting of a fuel tank filled with jellied gasoline was armed by attaching a hand grenade to the fuel cap. When dropped, the pin would be pulled, thus arming the weapon. The ground crews became so efficient that they could rig a delayed reaction in three-minute intervals. This delay allowed the jellied gasoline to spread prior to explosion for maximum effect.

Increased effectiveness of the Black Widow was the goal of all the night fighter squadrons. Like the 425th in Europe, the 550th, 548th and 419th night fighter squadrons in the Pacific also modified their aircraft to carry 5 in. HVARs (high velocity aircraft rockets). In mid-March 1945 Capt. John Striebel joined the 550th NFS at Morotai. Captain Striebel was not a newcomer to night fighter operations. He had served with the RAF in Europe flying Mosquitos prior to his coming to the SWPA. He also participated in P-38 night fighter evaluations back in the States, gaining invaluable experience.

On Striebel's suggestion, rockets were used in the squadron's intruder missions. An intensive search commenced for the required equipment to make the necessary modifications on the squadron P-61s. The men of the 550th Night Fighter Squadron obtained this required equipment through "cooperation with nearby Naval units." By early June, all the 550th aircraft had been so modified and from their new base at Tacloban on Leyte commenced operations against Japanese forces within their radius of operations.

Both in the field and back at the Northrop factory at Hawthorne, California, experiments were going on to evaluate the flying qualities of the P-61 while carrying the large 310 gallon fuel tanks instead of the much smaller 165 gallon tanks. In the Pacific, both the 419th and 550th carried out such experiments and found that the P-61 flew much the same with either tank. First Lt. Robert A. Frenzel, squadron test pilot for the 419th NFS, test flew their initial P-61 equipped with two of the 310 gallon droppable auxiliary fuel tanks.

Tests proved that the P-61 could take off in less than 3,000 ft., handled and flew normally with the noticeable weight increase. Eleven hours of economic cruising was calculated as the aircraft's maximum time. One difficulty was encountered, though, when the 310 gallon tanks were dropped: the wing flaps sustained slight damage. With the extended range of the 310 gallon auxiliary tanks, the 419th also improved the accuracy of their rocket-firing P-61s with the addition of AN/APN-1 radar altimeters for greater safety while flying in zero-visibility weather.

One of the few joint night fighter operations in the Pacific was the support of the Allied invasion of Balikpapan on the east coast of Borneo in late June 1945. Detachments from the 418th, 419th and 550th night fighter squadrons staged out of Sanga Sanga in the Sulu Archipelago. The 550th was the first to arrive, on June 1, with the 419th and 418th following later that same month. Their missions were preinvasion intruder strikes and night patrol over the task force between June 21 and 30 at which time Navy carrier planes took over intruder strikes and cover of the landings and night ground-support missions. During their stay, the 419th NFS's aircraft fitted with 310 gallon auxiliary fuel tanks flew no less than 107 missions. Not to be surpassed, the 550th NFS dispensed a total of thirty-two 5 in. HVAR and high-explosive rockets on a single day in early July.

Iwo Jima Area

The night fighter squadrons of the Seventh Air Force were not remaining idle either, for they were following the Allies through another part of the Pacific. The Allies invaded Iwo Jima on Feb. 19, 1945. Two days later a detachment of the 6th Night Fighter Squadron, which was giving night cover to Saipan, sent a flight of aircraft to Iwo Jima to provide night air defense for the newly won airfield, and to give night support to the Allied forces in their drive to defeat the fanatical defenders of this strategic island. Seven days later the entire 548th NFS arrived on Iwo Jima to give their support. This was the first time the entire 548th had seen combat. Prior to this, only a detachment had seen any combat while stationed along with the 6th detachment on Saipan. The remain-

der of the squadron provided night defense for the Hawaiian Islands.

The 549th, which had arrived some two weeks after the 548th, would remain on Iwo Jima until end of hostilities and saw little aerial combat, laying claim to only one aerial kill. With the entire 548th and 549th night fighter squadrons on Iwo Jima, the 6th NFS's detachment returned to Kagman Field on Saipan to provide another couple of weeks night cover prior to returning to Kipapa, Hawaii, where they rejoined the squadron and prepared for Operation Olympic.

Widow Versus Jug on Ie Shima

Okinawa was the Allies' next big move. The invasion commenced on Apr. 1, 1945; the fighting was bitter and intense. It wasn't until mid-June that the island was considered secure. The 548th NFS moved from their Iwo Jima base to Ie Shima, a small island off the coast of Okinawa on June 8.

Enemy aircraft were not the only ones over which the Widow had to prove itself superior. While in the Ryukyus (islands southwest of Japan), the 548th was under the 318th Fighter Group

Here with a P-61 named Sleepy Time Gal *is R/O Lieutenant Condren of the 549th NFS.* Louis Alford

63

commanded by Lt. Col. Harry C. McAfee. The 548th had an Officer's Club that was frequented by the 318th's CO and his friends. Besides enjoying the liquor at the club, the men of the 318th enjoyed poking fun at the 548th, using such snide remarks as "bomber pilots." Col. Dave Curtis, CO of the Black Widow boys, eventually became fed up with this

The insignia of the 549th NFS.

continuous ribbing and announced that he could outdo McAfee and his P-47N with his trusty P-61.

Colonel Curtis told the story this way:

"His response was an offer to 'load up the guns, and we'll go up and have it out!'

"Though alcohol was an active ingredient in the situation, reason eventually prevailed. His bet with me was $700 to be decided by superiority in two of three competitions. (1) Shortest takeoff roll. (2) Top speed in level flight to be done on the deck over the ocean to preclude cheating by diving. (3) Simulated air-to-air combat with gun cameras for documentation.

"In due time the contest started. His Jug was stripped of all reasonably removable weight, including guns and armor plate; I don't know what else. I reduced my ammo load to 20 rounds of 20 mm. The word had gotten around. A crowd of many hundreds had collected and many thousands of dollars were to change owners. The two aircraft lined up, wing tip to wing tip.

"He ran power up to full bore with

water injection (2,800 hp) and released brakes. As the aircraft moved forward the tail wheel came up, then back down as the main gear lifted off. He literally hung it on the prop, with tail wheel rolling after the main gear lifted clear. I was impressed (as were many spectators who told me later they figured then that it was over except the pay off).

"My turn. Water injection (2x2,250 hp) and released the brakes. When the air speed showed 75 mph, I started the flaps down and lifted the nose to a steep climbing altitude. I had beaten him by 75 yards!

"In level flight we lined up again, tip-to-tip. At his nod we each turned 90 degrees in opposite directions; a minute later we each turned 180 degrees to come at each other near head on. It had been agreed we would break as we passed—then everything goes. Both of us turned as hard as we could, for a few moments it looked questionable. Then the greater maneuverability of the Black Widow began to show; I moved inexorably towards his tail. He dove sharply, but I remained behind him; but always staying higher (height is nearly always an advantage). Eventually I was right behind his tail, my camera whirling. 'Best two out of three,' was his radio call.

"Back up we went and again squared away. This time I pitched sharply up as we broke. In less than one turn I was grinning through my sights at an uncomfortably rotated face, 'Let's go home!'

"I had frames of gun film with nothing but Jug in them. Several claimed they could recognize the Colonel's panic filled face. They never came to our club again."

As the Widow showed its superiority over the Jug at Ie Shima, so were the Allies showing their superiority over the Japanese forces. The invasion of Japan, Operation Olympic, was in full preparation. The 6th NFS of Seventh Air Force was preparing in Hawaii, while the Fifth Air Force brought its 421st and 547th night fighter squadrons up from the Southwest Pacific Area to join the Seventh AF's 548th on Ie Shima in late July and early August, and the Fifth's 418th NFS arriving on Okinawa in late July 1945. This left the Thirteenth Air Force's 419th and 550th to provide defense and support for the forces in the Philippine Islands at Puerto Princesa on Palawan and Tacloban on Leyte, respectively.

Members of A flight at Ie Shima, pictured with the second and final version of Bat Out'A Hell, *a P-61 piloted by flight leader*

Capt. William Dames. Bob Boucher via Warren Thompson

From their bases on Okinawa and Ie Shima, the night fighters flew night intruder missions to Japan's southern island of Kyushu.

The crew of 2nd Lt. Jerry D. Laubly, pilot, and his crew, 2nd Lt. Leonard S. Frumer (R/O) and Sgt. John H. Loring, gunner, joined the 418th NFS on Okinawa on July 25, 1945. A few days later they flew their first long-range mission to Japan, which was relatively uneventful. While returning to base, however, they strayed too close to US Navy ships and were fired at. With much maneuvering, Laubly managed to evade the flack and felt it was time to reassure his R/O that all was well. He found this impossible, though, as he observed his R/O floating downward toward the blue Pacific Ocean (Frumer thought they had had it and bailed out). He was picked up within hours and rejoined the squadron a few days later. Frumer took the inevitable kidding with remarkable good nature, for he and everyone else knew that it was a natural thing to happen to an R/O out of the States only two weeks. The 418th Night Fighter Squadron history which recalled this incident said about Laubly, "He has proven himself many times since."

Last Aerial Victory

Skip-bombing, rocket firing and long-range intruder missions were all part of their preparation for Operation Olympic. However, the last aerial kill of the war required not one shot. What was probably the last kill before V-J Day is credited to the 548th NFS operating from Ie Shima. It was on the night of Aug. 14, 1945, the day Japan agreed to surrender. That night Lt. Robert W. Clyde and his R/O Lt. Bruce K. LeFord had the alert duty. GCI picked up a bogey and at 2145 hours, lieutenants Clyde and LeFord were in their P-61 *Lady in the Dark* and lifting off the runway. At about 2200 hours, LeFord made initial contact on his radar set. Visual identification followed soon after—it was an Oscar. In the ensuing minutes the Widow made numerous attempts to get in firing position. Each time the wary Oscar managed to escape the *Lady* with violent evasive maneuvers. The chase came down to white-cap level. In an attempt to evade the pursuer, the Oscar crashed into the Pacific. This Widow made the last kill not with its tremendous firepower, but by the enemy's fear of what he knew the craft could do.

The night fighters were in to the very end. In the early afternoon hours of Aug. 19, 1945, the sky over Ie Shima filled with hundreds of P-38s and numerous B-25s crisscrossing the skies as two white Japanese Betty bombers prepared to land. These aircraft were not attacking but bringing the Japanese peace emissary on their way to meet with General MacArthur. At Ie Shima, the Japanese transferred from their aircraft to Air Transport Command C-54s which took them to Manila in the Philippines to discuss the Japanese capitulation. Upon their return to Ie Shima, the Japanese transferred from their aircraft to the Bettys. It was nearing darkness. As part of their escort back to the Japanese mainland, the Bettys, of which only one made a successful takeoff, had two Widows of the 421st Night Fighter Squadron. These aircraft were piloted by Gerald A. Parker and Robert E. Savaria. Eighteen years later on Aug. 23, 1963, Savaria would lose his life while flying a P-61 in another type of battle. This time against forest fires on the Tule River Indian Reservation in central California.

The insignia of the 548th NFS.

Jap-Batty, a P-61 piloted by Lt. Jerome M. Hanson of the 6th NFS. Hanson is credited with one Betty damaged and another destroyed. Left to right is Ray Mooney (R/O), Jerome Hanson (pilot), Dale Haberman (pilot), William Wallace (R/O), Francis Eaton (pilot) and James Ketchum (R/O) after being awarded Air Medals for the destruction of an enemy aircraft by each of these Black Widow crews. USAF

Chapter 6

Night Action over Europe

The beginning of a new year, 1944, found the Ninth Air Force still in the throes of building up to full strength. It had been transferred from the Mediterranean theater to the European theater just the previous October. Among the

Crew chief T. Sgt Joe Moe of the 422nd NFS beside his pinup gal on the nose wheel on the P-61 Borrowed Time. AAF

new units to arrive was the 422nd Night Fighter Squadron. The future of the 422nd, as well as its two sister squadrons (the 423rd and 425th) which were to follow in the next two months, was quite uncertain.

With the distinction of being the first operational USAAF night fighter squadron to receive training in the P-61 Black Widow, the 422nd were somewhat surprised to find no aircraft available

when they arrived at Charmy Down, England, on Mar. 7, 1944. It would be some time before they would receive their Widows, about two and a half months. Unknown to these night fighters, much behind the scenes action was taking place.

In the Pacific, the American night fighters had found the P-70 useless. The four USAAF Beaufighter-equipped squadrons in the Mediterranean were

The 414th NFS was the first of four Mediterranean AAF night fighter squadrons to turn in their British equipment for the P-61. Receiving the Widow in December 1944, they *and the 415th NFS would be the only two to use the Widow during the war. The 416th and 417th would not change until after the war. The Beautiful Ass, a 414th NFS P-61,* *sports a swimsuit-attired female riding a donkey. USAF*

also finding their craft outmatched by the opposition. Demand for the very promising P-61 was quite great. But it had its problems, too, and production had fallen behind. To help alleviate these problems, the AAF started negotiations with the British to obtain Mosquito night fighters.

The Mosquito

As of late 1943 the AAF had decided that the P-61 was more desirable than the Mosquito for the Pacific units, and that the ETO (European theater of operations) and MTO (Mediterranean theater of operations) forces should receive the Mosquito. In early December, Lt. Col. J. A. Gibbs of Operations, Commitments, and Requirements (OC&R) Section, Requirements Division, Fighter & Air Defense Branch created a proposed allocation for Mosquito aircraft to USAAF night fighter squadrons that was to be presented to the British during negotiations. It called for the AAF's MTO night fighter force to receive thirty-four Mosquitos initially. Under this arrangement, the Beaufighters of the AAF's four underequipped squadrons would be reallocated to two of the squadrons and the remaining two squadrons would be reequipped with the Mosquito. The plan then called for eight Mosquitos per month to be delivered over the next twelve months. These latter deliveries were to reequip the two Beaufighter squadrons and to replace lost Mosquitos.

The three American squadrons scheduled for commitment to the ETO as of Feb. 1, Apr. 1 and May 1, 1944, were each to receive a full complement of eighteen Mosquitos as initial equipment, and two replacement craft per month for the rest of the year.

But the Mosquito was having its own production problems. In a communique dated Jan. 21, 1944, to Maj. Gen. Barney M. Giles (chief of the Air Staff, HQ AAF), Air Chief Marshal Courtney states:

"I believe I may have inadvertently misled you as to the date when the four US squadrons can be reequipped from Beaufighters to Mosquitos. The position is that a number of British Night Fighter Squadrons in the UK are still equipped with the Beaufighter, and I believe you would agree that they should have priority over squadrons in the Mediterranean theatre. The Mosquito night fighters are coming through very slowly, and I am afraid that it will not be possible to begin the reequipment of the Mediterranean squadrons until the second half of the year. In the meantime,

In July 1944 Northrop held a "Name a Black Widow" contest for two Black Widows purchased by Northrop employees (Norcrafters) in the Fifth War Loan Bond Drive. Albin A.

Johnson's winning suggestion was First Nighter. *Johnson picked this name because it was the name of his favorite radio program.*

A close-up of the 414th NFS's First Nighter *reveals the frequently used artwork better known as* Sleepy Time Gal. *This artwork was inspired by the Vargas girls popular during that period. Bomb mission markings on*

First Nighter *are for missions made possible by the ingenuity of the night fighter squadrons. By attaching P-38 bomb shackles to the fuselage and wing pylons, the P-61 could carry three 1,000 lb. bombs.*

however, we can maintain the squadrons with Beaufighters."

Generals Giles and Ira C. Eaker (commanding general, Mediterranean Allied Air Forces) and Air Marshal Jack Slessor later discussed this matter and concurred in the fact that the AAF night fighters in the MTO should be maintained even at the expense of "rolling up" some of the RAF night fighter squadrons there. On February 7 the AAF decided to cancel all P-61 commitments to the MTO and rely on RAF support to the MTO Beaufighter squadrons. Apparently in January, General Giles and Air Marshal W. L. Welsh had come to an agreement on Mosquito requirements for the first six months of 1944, and a tentative agreement for the remainder of the year. By the end of May, not a single Mossie night fighter had been delivered, and slippage in production schedule and British home defense requirements made near-term delivery virtually impossible.

The A-20J Havoc

Ninth Air Force's IX Tactical Air Command received its second night fighter squadron when the 423rd joined the 422nd at Charmy Down on Apr. 17, 1944. Fresh from the newly established California night fighter training establishment they, like their predecessor squadron, were eager to show their adeptness at night fighting. Unlike the 422nd, however, they would soon receive their operational steeds.

The aircraft the 423rd received, and the change in their mission, were quite a shock at first. They were to fly A-20J Havocs and were to perform the role of night photographic squadron. On May 18 they were transferred from IX Tactical Air Command to the 10th Photographic Reconnaissance Group, and two days later they left Charmy Down and moved to Chalgrove Airdrome in Oxon. A few days later, four crews from the 33rd PRS (10th PRG) were assigned to the 423rd on detached service to train the 423rd in night photography.

During this period, the 423rd's A-20J aircraft were modified to carry K19 vertical cameras and flash-bomb racks in the bomb bay. Some of their aircraft were equipped with an electronic flash lamp. These lamps, which were developed by Dr. Harold Edgerton of MIT (Massachusetts Institute of

Technology), were good for almost an unlimited number of flashes.

The squadron's first operational mission was flown during the early hours of D-day. Four crews were dispatched to photograph German troop movements in six target areas on the Cherbourg peninsula; all crews made it back to base. One crew that had an A-20J equipped with the Edgerton lamp achieved the best results. The other crews had some difficulty with their

Pictured here is a nameless lady of the 414th.

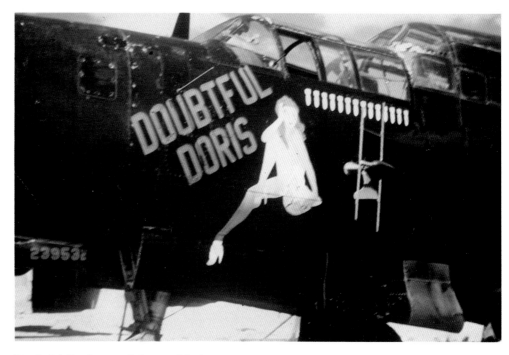

Doubtful Doris *posed here with its many bomb mission strikes, and by contrast with other 414th aircraft was quite provocative.*

69

flash bombs in timing and altitude. On June 22, 1944, the 423rd Night Fighter Squadron was redesignated the 155th Photographic Reconnaissance Squadron.

The Black Widow Arrives

Movement was in the wind. The 422nd received warning orders for an impending move in early May. With bags packed, they made the actual trek on the sixth. Their new station was Scorton, England. Much to their liking, there were numerous AAF and RAF aircraft that would be at their disposal for flight, navigation and AI training.

Also to their liking were rumors concerning P-61s having arrived in England. To find out for himself, their CO, Col. Oris B. Johnson, along with Capts. Edward S. Page and George W. Reynolds, and Lt. Ernest P. Luke (intelligence, operations and engineering officers, respectively) flew to Speke on May 10. It was true! Lined up on the field were

eight olive-drab-over-gray P-61A-5s. With a little coaxing from Colonel Johnson, their craft were given a high priority with a promise that the aircraft would be ready around the twentieth of May.

These were not the first Widows to reach England, though. Just about a month and a half earlier, a P-61A-1, serial number 42-5496, was delivered to the RAF for their evaluation. Their interest in this aircraft was not surprising, for its design initiation had been brought about by a British design request given to Northrop. It is also interesting to note that fifty of the first fifty-seven production aircraft were initially scheduled for Lend Lease.

The first Black Widow arrived at Scorton on May 23, thus the 422nd became the third AAF night fighter squadron to be equipped with this aircraft. It had been seventy-seven long days since the 422nd arrived in Great Britain, and morale had never been as high as it was this day. The rest of the

month and early June was spent getting reacquainted with the Black Lady. The RAF loaned experienced night fighter personnel to aid in the Yanks' tutoring; the American R/Os hadn't looked at a radar scope since Christmas. Because these aircraft were not equipped with turrets, all gunners were transferred to other units, mainly the A-20-equipped 423rd NFS.

Possibly due to RAF influence, or lessons already learned by the Americans on their own, the 422nd decided that an all-over glossy-black paint scheme was superior to the olive-drab-over-gray garb that their craft arrived in. To perform the painting task, a nearby RAF unit was contacted. Their choice of colors, which probably weren't part of the original bargain, varied and apparently the crews picked whatever color tickled their fancy.

James F. Postlewaite III of the 422nd NFS recalled:

"We got all our noses sprayed on an RAF base in England; they being the radar kings. They sprayed lead to the underside of the radome to reduce the ground scatter out of the radar. Our radar was pretty sensitive, and this would take out the clutter from the ground. Well, everybody had different colors—some had red, brick red noses. You'd have this lead bottom, and then the fellow would ask you what you wanted for a paint job. I've forgotten who started this. We happened to go in one day, and he didn't have too many dark colors. All he had were the light ones, so we took the yellow one and away we went. It was quite outstanding. When we brought it back, I thought O. B. [Col. Oris B.] Johnson (squadron CO) was just gonna flip. Oh, you could see that airplane 20 miles away in the sky in the daytime. And do you know at night, in the black night, I've run into that airplane. I couldn't see it, and I've run right in and smacked my head on it.

"As it turned out, things weren't so bad. I flew wing for O. B. Johnson one of our first times we pulled the maneuver of taking off before the day fighters came back. Well, it was real great, about 4,000 ft. you know, that's a real tight formation. He was screaming about that yellow nose as we were headed towards Germany before the sunset. I didn't feel any better about it than he did because you could see us coming. That night he

Sleepy Time Gal *with members of the 422nd NFS. In the center is actor Mickey Rooney. While visiting the troops, he got into the* spirit of things and dressed as a member of the crew. AFM

70

stirred five of them up. I chased them all over the Bonn airdrome, and we didn't even get to see one; but I got the green light at Bonn airdrome from the tower to land. We wanted to catch them in the landing pattern; it had been one of their tactics to shoot Allied airplanes in the landing approach with the wheel in the down position, when you're sort of helpless. They had no lights, no nothing, and were sinking. They were probably Fw 190s and were going fast, but we never saw them."

The Ninth Air Force's third night fighter squadron, the 425th NFS, arrived at Charmy Down on May 26, 1944. Their CO, Lt. Col. Leon G. "Gilly" Lewis, was a veteran of the southwest Pacific theater, having flown combat missions against the Japanese in Martin B-26s between February 1942 and July 1943. Inactivity was relatively short for the 425th, however. On June 12 they were transplanted to Scorton and started checking out in their P-61s.

It would seem that some forces, other than the operational night fighter people, still wanted the Mosquito. Both of the Ninth Air Force night fighter squadrons had the Widow for less than a month and had not flown a combat mission yet when Gen. Carl Spaatz wired Gen. Henry H. "Hap" Arnold on June 13, 1944:

"Tests have indicated P-61 will not prove satisfactory night fighter against most German night bombers presently used primarily because of speed limitation. Vandenberg is worried that Ninth Air Force may not be able to take over night defense at scheduled time because of this limitation. It has been suggested that water injection and 150 grade fuel may improve this situation. If this is impractical or does not allow sufficient improvement, information is requested as to the possibility of procuring sufficient late-model Canadian built Mosquitos for substitution in night fighter units. Should this be possible, request an estimate of delay caused by training and modification (training air ground crews) on this type airplane."

The following day, Arnold sent a reply stating that water injection was being introduced already on the aircraft being produced (P-61A-10), which gave

Impatient Widow, *a P-61 of the 422nd NFS, was damaged in combat with an He 177 the evening of Aug. 14, 1944. Its right engine and hydraulic system were shot out. The He 177 got away but not without being hit.* Stegner

a minimal increase in performance of 10 mph, and that 150 grade aviation gasoline (avgas) had not been tested stateside. Arnold also stated that the Canadian Mosquitoes were of the "unarmed bomber type," and that modification to night fighter configuration would require extensive modification. Negotiations "with the British Air Commission to secure 36 British built Mosquito night fighters for your two squadrons" were in process, however, according to the reply.

Oblivious to the Mosquito/Widow controversy at the higher echelons, the night fighters were doing a good job of preparing themselves and their craft for combat. A unique modification made by the 425th Night Fighter Squadron to their Black Widows was the relocation of the R/O's equipment from the rear of the crew nacelle to the gunner's compartment (their aircraft were without turrets). Exactly how the idea came about is uncertain, but apparently the squadron liked the side-by-side pilot-R/O arrangement in the British Mosquito. They also felt strongly about having another pair of eyes up front. Northrop technical representative Rulon V. Harmon, along with the squadron's engineering and radar officers, and Capt. Russell Glasser, a squadron pilot and the only graduate mechanical engineer in the unit, made a mock-up installation out of cardboard in one of the P-61s. Russ Glasser recalls how the project progressed:

"We drew up plans for the changeover and went up to Ninth Air Force to propose the change. They were turned down because Ninth felt that the airplanes could not be kept out of commission long enough to make the conversion, being needed for combat missions that were scheduled. They felt that the change was not worth the time and money required. The 425th disagreed and went on with their plans. I checked with the engineering officer at Burtonwood, a major repair depot in England. They agreed, but the plane needed a reason to be down for about two days. I scheduled time, promising that they would have a valid reason to keep the airplane down that long.

"So when it became time to have the props magnafluxed (required every 50 hours) on my plane, I flew it to Burtonwood. I came in for a landing about 50 ft. too high, did what was an apparent stall, caught it just before it hit the ground and made what to me was a normal landing but to the control tower it looked practically like a crash landing. I then called the tower and asked if everything looked all right. They said it looked like I was minus one piece of the airplane and should have it checked. So I wrote up a Form 5 stating that it needed a landing gear strut and wing examination and had it towed into the hangar.

"While the props were being magnafluxed, we installed the radar equipment in the gunner's position. The change increased the speed, depending on the airplane, from 15 to 20 mph at cruise, the center of gravity was changed 15 in. forward, the angle of flight at cruise was changed from a slightly nose up to a slight nose down attitude. It made a remarkable difference.

"We then persuaded the chief engineering officer from Ninth Air Force to fly both the converted and regular models. He then authorized the change. He was so impressed that he completely forgot the circumstances under which the conversion had been made."

By mid-June the squadrons were nearing operational readiness. Col. Oris B. Johnson of the 422nd made arrangements with an RAF Halifax unit at Croft, England, to engage with the 422nd NFS in day and night practice intercept missions called Bull's Eye. These exercises provided needed practice for both the bomber crews in evasive action against theoretical Luftwaffe night fighters, and aided the Americans in working out night attack tactics against bombers. These tactics are described fully in the 422nd's history:

"The daylight tactics were designed to give the 'Big Friends' a real workout in evasive tactics, but at the same time it piled up the time to the credit of the 'Blip Jockeys.' The night exercises ('Bull's Eye') were damn good practice. The Halifaxes would take off on a three-legged flight, covering the greater part of Northern England and Scotland. We were given an area to defend and GCI would vector us into the stream. 'Win-

Borrowed Time, *a P-61 of the 422nd NFS.* Stegner

dow' and evasive tactics were used by the bomber boys. When we got within minimum AI range and in position for the kill, we would so signal by flipping on the navigation lights, while the tail or other gunners flashed a light if they had us in their sights before our lights went on. Such was our success that it tended towards an underestimation of the Huns' abilities as well as a feeling of overconfidence on our part, best expressed by the remark, 'the number you shoot down on one sortie depends largely on how few rounds you have fired to make the kill.' Little dreams of glory, but it looked so easy. There must be a catch to it. Also, PIs (Practice Intercepts) were attempted with the target taking the most violent evasive action, which the Widows were capable of, and that was plenty. The stars over Yorkshire saw some rugged interceptions, but it was the best kind of practice."

The night fighters' ego was greatly deflated after a visit by Brig. Gen. William L. Richardson, commanding general of IX Air Defense Command, on June 21. They had come under his command just the day before. During his visit, the general left the impression that the night fighters would be subordinate to the antiaircraft units, and that their sole responsibility would be to protect areas and installations in the rear areas.

The P-61 Versus the Mosquito

The 422nd Night Fighter Squadron had received their first P-61s just thirty-five days earlier (the 425th had theirs for a shorter period), when on June 27, 1944, Col. Winston W. Kratz of the 481st Night Fighter Operational Training Group and Col. Henry Viccellio from the Fighter and Air Defense Branch of OC&R of the War Department arrived at Scorton. The purpose of colonels Kratz and Viccellio's trip was to determine the suitability of the P-61 for combat operations in the ETO, and the readiness of the 422nd and 425th night fighter squadrons.

A detachment of six P-61s—with three crews from the 422nd, two from the 425th and Colonel Kratz flying the sixth aircraft—was sent on temporary duty to Hurn Airdrome. This site was chosen due to its close proximity to the Normandy beachhead. While at Hurn, this composite detachment was attached to the 125th Newfoundland Squadron for their period of operational readiness and suitability evaluation. The 422nd's Col. Oris B. Johnson was placed in charge of the combat evaluation.

The "replace the P-61 with the Mosquito" forces had made themselves known to the night fighters, and the night fighters weren't happy. Jim Postlewaite of the 422nd remembers those days very well:

"We took our wings off and went into O. B. and laid them on the table and said, 'If we don't fly the '61, we all quit,' and walked out. Then we had to make a test between the '61 and the Mosquito. The Northrop technical representative took O.B.'s airplane and screwed the props down so they wouldn't fly off and put Norm Williams and [Donald] Doyle in as the crew. They went up and they took that Mosquito apart."

The P-61 did not only have to prove itself in combat against the Axis forces (which it did), but it also had to prove itself superior to Allied aircraft. The idea of changing from their newly acquired P-61s for Mosquitos did not sit well with the men of the night fighter squadrons, upon whose shoulders the fate of the Widow rested. The evaluation demonstration of the two aircraft took place on July 5, 1944, at RAF Station Hurn. The 422nd's unit history relates it this way:

"On the 5th, the long awaited test with a Mosquito (Mk. 17) was laid on at 1600. Squadron Leader Barnwell of 125 Squadron and his R/O versus Lt. Donald J. Doyle and F/O Norman N. Williams. The P-61 more than exceeded even our

The insignia of the 422nd NFS.

Lady Gen, *the top-scoring P-61 of the 422nd NFS. Pictured in the middle is Brig. Gen. Elwood "Pete" R. Quesada. On either side of the general are officers of the 422nd—all of whom are wearing the DFC.* Lady Gen *was piloted by Paul Smith. The R/O was Bob Tierney.* Stegner

wildest hopes, being faster at 5,000, 10,000, 15,000 and 20,000 ft.; outturned the Mossie at every altitude and by a big margin; and far surpassed the Mossie in rate of climb. We could go faster and slower up or down. Faster than the pride of the British—a most enjoyable afternoon!"

A memo to Lt. Gen. Hoyt S. Vandenburg, commanding officer of the Ninth Air Force, from Fighter and Air Defense Branch, OC&R, whose subject was the Report of Operational Test of the P-61, dated July 7, 1944, in the ETO, stated that the "Mosquito and P-61 were approximately equal in performance with the P-61 being slightly faster."

This was not the first time that the Black Widow had to meet the Mosquito in mock combat. Colonel Kratz was associated with the Widow in an earlier exercise and recounts its origin:

"I was in Lt. Gen. Carl Spaatz's office along with Mr. Robert A. Lovett, then assistant secretary of war for air. We wanted to know whether or not the

P-61 should be produced in quantity. Mr. Lovett was very much in favor of it; General Spaatz was not. He said he had the performance troops (at Eglin Field, Florida) in the P-61 and the Mosquito, and they had found the Mosquito to be better. He had arranged for the AAF to get 200 Mosquitos.

"I asked General Spaatz if he couldn't have a competition. I had an informal competition. I flew the P-61 and someone else flew the Mosquito, and we tried climbs, and so on. I was very elated at the results and sent back this report to General Spaatz. The P-61 was then mass produced. A couple of months later a more formal contest was held using test pilots. I'm sure they could get a great deal more out of the '61 than I could and probably a test pilot could get more out of a Mosquito. The same thing happened.

"I'm absolutely sure to this day that the British were lying like troopers. I honestly believe the P-61 was not as fast as the Mosquito. The British needed the

Mosquito because by that time it was the one airplane that could get into Berlin and back without getting shot down. I doubt very seriously that the others knew better. But come what may, the '61 was a good night fighter. In the combat game you've got to be pretty realistic about these things. The P-61 was not a superior night fighter. It was not a poor night fighter; it was a good night fighter. It did not have quite enough speed."

Chasing Buzz Bombs

It was settled; the P-61 would fly for the Ninth Air Force. Now the night fighters could get down to the business at hand—destroying the enemy. Operational orders were issued for a detachment of the 422nd Night Fighter Squadron to proceed to Ford Airdrome in mid-July to chase V-1 buzz bombs. This type of work was called anti-diver patrol. On their first night (July 15, 1944), pilot Lt. Herman E. Ernst and his R/O, Lt. Edward H. Kopsel, were vectored by GCI to an intercept position to meet incoming V-1s. In order for the P-61 to gain enough speed to intercept these speedy pilotless craft, it was now necessary to go into a slight dive—from behind. Ernst was on the attack, flying through clouds and on instruments, when his tail cone disintegrated.

The next night, July 16, Ernst and Kopsel were on patrol again, along with the crew of Capt. Robert O. Elmore and Lt. Leonard F. Mapes. Flying at 3,000 ft. Ernst spotted four V-1s approaching the English coastline. An interception was initiated on the first missile but had to be aborted due to an RAF Mosquito making an attack on the same buzz bomb. Ernst awaited the second buzz bomb and dived on it from 5,000 ft. With the V-1 flying at about 350 mph, the Widow closed in to 2,000 ft. before Ernst let loose with his first salvo. After closing within a 900 ft. range, he fired again; hits were observed on the robot's propulsion unit. It went into a steep dive and exploded prior to reaching the Channel.

Robert F. Graham, former R/O for the 422nd, reminisced: "I wish I could remember the name of the crew. They got in behind this buzz bomb off of Cherbourg. They were in perfect position; they slid in behind it, and the R/O was reading its range: '600 ft., 500 ft., 400 ft., shoot! 300 ft., 200 ft., aw forget it!' And about that time the pilot opened up. The

No Love, No Nothing II! *was piloted by Lt. Col. O. B. Johnson, CO of the 422nd. The first Widows delivered to the squadron were in the original olive drab over gray. It was* discovered through testing that the glossy-black planes were less visible in the night skies than the flat-black or olive-drab planes. Stegner

propulsion unit blew up. Boy, smoke and fire and everything else came out! When they got down to the ground, the R/O just looked at the pilot, turned his back on him and walked off."

The inward collapsing of the tail cone on Ernst's first mission was not uncommon among the early P-61s, and was experienced in all theaters. Field modifications were made to strengthen the plexiglass, while changes to eliminate this problem were made back in Hawthorne, California, at the Northrop factory.

The battle of the buzz bombs at Ford Airdrome had been in progress for less than two weeks when the 422nd received movement orders for the Continent. The crews liked the idea that the bombs didn't fire back at them, but there were other dangers. One night, Lt. Tadas J. Spelis and his R/O, Lt. Eleutherios "Lefty" Eleftherion, found this out the hard way. They, along with the squadron's intelligence officer, Lt. Philip M. Guba, flying in the gunner's seat, intercepted an incoming bomb. The attack was pressed hard, and they were about 450 ft. from the craft when it exploded.

At such close range the P-61 was thrown out of control and bounced around like a tiny ship at sea in a storm. With much effort, Spelis regained enough control to get them safely back to base. An inspection of the aircraft showed both ailerons badly scorched; the fabric on the left rudder and left half of the elevator was burned away while the other half of the elevator and right rudder were badly scorched; plus miscellaneous holes and dents all over on the plane.

Moving to the Continent

The Allies were pushing the Germans away from the French coast, and IX Tactical Air Command, to which the 422nd NFS was assigned, was following the First Army and providing coordinated support. The main body of the 422nd NFS arrived at the captured German airfield at Maupertuis, near Cherbourg, France, in late July. The last Widows and crew arrived on July 31, 1944. Col. Leon G. Lewis' 425th arrived on the Continent on Aug. 12, 1944, and got into action immediately. Colonel Lewis remembered:

"We had just moved to the Brittany peninsula between Lorient and St.

Little Audrey *with the lady for whom the plane was named, and members of the 422nd NFS.* Stegner

Moonlight Wreck-Wizishun *has just received the nose of another P-61,* Wacky Wabbit. *The ground crews became quite good at their jobs of repair and maintenance while in the fields. They worked under sometimes very harsh conditions, but managed to keep the planes in the air.* Stegner

Nazaire. Flew in one afternoon; the Germans had left that morning. They had not destroyed anything. The Third Army had Lorient and St. Nazaire encircled, a couple of German divisions in each one. The Germans broke out shortly thereafter and tried to connect up; there was no airpower available to intervene. One of the armored divisions sent a major over to ask if we could provide air support. We had no radio communications with higher command, so I had to turn him down. Then a colonel came over and we went through the same routine. He was quite pushed out of shape over the turn-down. Then a Major General came over and convinced me I should supply the air support. We put up a maximum ground-support effort (pilots flying only). We hit a German tank column trying to link up with others. We were able to turn them back by making daylight runs straight down their throats. Each plane made two passes. We lost our first aircraft and pilot on this mission. I finally established communications with HQ shortly thereafter, and they relieved me of command right on the spot. I went before a general board the day after and was reinstated after explaining the circumstances."

Lts. Paul A. Smith and Robert E. Tierney of the 422nd made an intercept on an unidentified plane in the late hours of August 6 that Tierney had on his scope; it was mandatory that positive visual identification be made before a shot was fired. Smith was trying to get close enough to identify it. By the time the craft was recognized as an Me 110, the German had realized he was in trouble. The Messerschmitt initiated evasive action. The 110 tried to turn away from the Black Widow, but the Americans stayed with him. Before long they were both standing on their wing tips, with the crews looking at each other as they pivoted in the blackness. Wings clashed and both craft went out of control momentarily. By the time Smith had his P-61 under control, the

Tactless Texan *is being hoisted from the ground after a crash-landing.* Stegner

German crew was gone. The paint on the Widow's wing leading edge had scrapings from the Messerschmitt.

The 422nd ended their stay at Maupertuis with a score of 3-4-1 (confirmed-probable-damaged), with the first kill going to the team of Lts. Raymond A. Anderson and John U. Morris when they destroyed a Ju 88 the night after Smith and Tierney's hair-raising escapade with the Me 110. At the end of August, the 422nd NFS left the activity on the Cherbourg peninsula for an uneventful and short stay at Chateaudun, France.

With the advance of the Allies, the various tactical air commands of the Ninth Air Force were assigned to support given armies. The XIX Tactical Air Command, which included the 422nd NFS, was placed in the support of Gen. George Patton's Third Army, and the XXIX TAC, which included the 425th NFS, provided tactical assistance for the Ninth Army.

Train Busting

Train busting was a major part of the 425th NFS's repertoire. One moonlit night Capt. Earl W. Bierer and his R/O, Lt. James Lothrop, Jr., were "stooging" around near Berlin. Spotting a train, Captain Bierer pulled back on the control column and wheeled over into a dive. He pressed the attack home and saw the engine explode and the rest of the train jump the tracks and pile, in a burning mass, into a ditch that ran parallel to the tracks.

With enough fuel and ammo left, the night fighter crew continued their patrol. Down a ways from their first encounter, they came upon two trains that were about to meet on a double set of tracks. Bierer swung his Widow out wide in order to come down at the point where he judged the two engines would pass, in hopes of getting both at one pass. Cutting over hard, he started lining up for his first victim. Brilliant puffs of orange and red flack came streaming up at the night intruder from both trains. It wasn't long before the P-61 was in position and going in for the kill. With all four 20 mm cannons in the Widow's belly blazing away, one train's engine was destroyed, the second train derailed. Many cars were ablaze with dead and wounded German soldiers; the Americans flew away unscathed.

By mid-September 1944, the 422nd NFS wound up their operations from Chateaudun and moved north to Florennes, Belgium, where the mud seemed to never dry up on that rainy, wind-torn field. As the year wore on, the weather deteriorated over most of the European continent, which drastically curtailed the operations of the "day" boys but served to increase the scope of the night fighter operations. Tactical, reconnaissance and intruder missions were initiated while their normal aerial defense duties continued. The night fighters had pleaded and would continue to do so through the remainder of the year with very little results for the required parts to modify their P-61, to enable them to carry external fuel tanks and ordnance.

Widows over Germany

One night, Lt. William A. Andrews and his R/O, Lt. James E. Kleinheinz (425th NFS) were flying an armed recon/intruder mission over Saarbrucken, Germany, when the lights of a German convoy caught their attention. In their desperation to get badly needed reinforcements to the battle zone, the Germans felt that the greater speed that could be obtained by using their headlights at night greatly outweighed the chance of being spotted by a night-flying Allied aircraft. The night fighters circled the vehicles as they got into position for the attack. With the trucks lined up, the P-61 roared the length of the whole line with its 20 mm cannons spitting projectiles of death and destruction. The night sky was lit up by the blaze of burning fuel and exploding ammunition.

On the night of October 13, Lts. Herman E. Ernst and Edward H. Kopsel were on a patrol mission southeast of Aachen, Germany, when they observed the first German jet at night. They believed the aircraft to be an Me 262. A few nights later Capt. Robert O. Elmore and his R/O, Lt. Leonard F. Mapes, made

After Tactless Texan *was raised, a tracking gear was wedged under the engine nacelle to* *make it mobile and ready for repairs.* Stegner

contact with an Me 163 rocket-propelled fighter. They chased the elusive craft in a circular pattern for two or three minutes before Elmore lost the 163 in a cloud.

A number of stories have come out about the Germans flying captured American aircraft. The USAAF night fighters have come up against German-flown B-17s, a B-24 and a Beaufighter. Jim Postlewaite of the 422nd had one such encounter: "I ran intercept one night on a B-17 with a swastika painted on its tail. It was just floating around, and I almost ran into him—that's why I saw it. I throttled back; we were boring in on him and flew by. You could see that ol' swastika painted on it. I asked the ground control what they wanted to do, and they said to let him go so we did."

The 422nd and 425th made their presence known by destroying Axis forces in the skies and on the ground. Single-handed, the night fighter team of Lts.

Paul A. Smith and Robert E. Tierney destroyed an entire German town in a roundabout fashion. They had successfully intercepted an He 111 and shot it down—all in a day's work for the night fighters—but it hit in the main road of a German village. As it slid down the main street, it systematically set each building on fire, destroying the entire town.

Battle damage is always a good probability when engaging the enemy—a calculated risk. Robert F. "Shorty" Graham of the 422nd can attest to this:

"I had a chance to bail out and didn't take it. One time we came back and couldn't get the right main gear down. Had a bad mission anyway. The weather was bad, and we were getting shy of fuel. We got back to the base, and the right main gear wouldn't come down. We tried and tried; shook it, stomped on it and everything. Bolinder [Lt. Robert G.] asked, 'You want to bail out?' I asked, 'What are you going to do?'

He said he was going to work with it a little longer. So I told him to just let me know when he was going to bail out. We messed around and finally we got it to indicate down and made normal approach, touchdown, and rolled about 100 ft. and it folded.

"We dug the wing in, went down the runway and came to rest out in the middle of an area that hadn't been demined yet. We sat there with the dust floating around. The fuel could be heard running out of the tanks; they had ruptured. I wanted a cigarette so bad I could taste it, but I didn't dare light one. I reached back and dropped the hatch. It barely moved before it hit the ground. I couldn't get out so I tried the top escape hatch. We'd had the planes painted several times experimenting with different colors for anti-searchlight work. In all this time it hadn't been opened with all those coats of paint. I butted it open with my head; I can still feel it. I got out

Tabitha, a P-61A-10, serial number 42-5569, of the 425th NFS seen here on the hardstand at Scorton, England, in 1944.

78

on top of the plane and then I didn't dare get off."

Battle of the Bulge

During the last month of the year, the 425th NFS in France was deeply involved in offensive missions, having modified their Widows to carry 5 in. high-velocity aircraft rockets. The rockets gave them the capability to do great damage against railroads, stock, motor transport and fixed facilities during a period of limited action against the Luftwaffe. One of the 425th's crews performing nocturnal ground attacks were Lieutenants Alvin E. Anderson (pilot) and John G. Smith (R/O). "Bud" Anderson recalled one of these hair-raising missions:

"I remember one night my radar operator and I were flying patrol at about 13,000 ft. when we saw what we thought was a convoy about 15 miles east of us. I had forgotten that my radar operator, Smith, had a head cold. In fact, he shouldn't have been flying—that's how it was in those days. I got permission from GCI to go down and attack. I split-Sed from about 13,000 ft. and headed across the target at a hell of a speed, descending to between 500 and 100 ft. My guns were blazing and my radar operator was screaming (his head was about ready to blow up because of his cold). I couldn't line up the ring and dot sight. I saw what I was coming into was a railroad yard so I just kicked the rudder back and forth spraying the whole area with 20s.

"Then I chandelled up at the end of the run to lose speed and made the turn to come back over the target again. I started my run back at about 150 mph and put down one-quarter flaps to get a better firing angle. Now we could see that we had started a number of fires in the railroad marshalling yard on our initial pass. We had four locomotives blowing steam from everywhere, and they had left the headlights on one engine. I decided to concentrate on that one. The fact is I had our plane trimmed up for cruise at 13,000 ft. at 220 or 240 mph. When I came across at 150 mph, I had to hold a hell of a lot of rudder and had difficulty keeping the ring and dot sight on the engine's headlight. I kept on correcting and shooting all the time.

"Well, I became so damned interested in lining up with the sight—I'm

shooting short bursts all the time—my R/O was observing over my shoulder [the 425th was the only unit to move the R/O from the rear of the crew nacelle to the gunner's position in their turretless P-61s], and he screamed over the intercom, 'pull up, you dumb son-of-a-bitch.' This jarred me enough so that I realized what I was doing [target fixation]. I pulled up sharply, putting on full throttle at the same time. Just after we pulled up over the locomotive, it blew up, creating a tremendous turbulence. We went up like an elevator. We climbed to 10,000 ft. and got a fix from GCI in order to spot the location as we didn't have the foggiest idea where we were. We could see the fires and the steam all over the area of the marshalling yard. The next day they sent out the photo reconnaissance. It turned out we were at Kaiserslautern marshalling yard. The photo recon verified five damaged/destroyed locomotives plus other miscellaneous damage. That was a pretty good night."

December 1944 was a month of remarkably good weather. Another noticeable fact was the apparent absence of the Luftwaffe. Unbeknownst to the 422nd night fighters was that by mid-December, they would be at the apex of

Gen. von Rundstedt's Ardennes counteroffensive—the Battle of the Bulge! The 422nd wanted to increase their offensive work against the Germans due to the lack of air action. In late November, "Bomber Command" of the "422nd Air Force" was formed when a number of war-weary A-20s were received. The squadron's historical report describes these aircraft quite vividly:

"When the seven wrecks did arrive, their condition gave food for some sober thought—one was a veteran of ninety missions. None were equipped with oxygen and all were pretty well beaten up."

For the first five days of the month, crews checked out in these aircraft and worked out a system of radar bombing with Marmite (GCI) control. Their first operational mission was on Dec. 5, 1944, when a leaflet drop was made between Julich and Linnich, Germany.

Soon the weather worsened and operations were curtailed. By December 15 the squadron had claimed only one enemy aircraft destroyed and one damaged. Then on the night of Dec. 16, 1944, the 422nd found themselves in the middle of something big. It started out as most nights did, but as time went on many people sensed an uneasy feeling.

The armorers' work was an endless task. In this photo are two armorers loading 20 mm ammo in preparation for a sortie.

Sightings of flares, increased night activities by unidentified aircraft, aircraft flying with their navigation lights on and lights on the ground were being reported increasingly to combat operations. The first to score on this very active night was the crew of Lts. Robert G. Bolinder and Robert F. Graham, who were flying on patrol between the Allied lines and the Rhine River. The 422nd history described the action thus:

"After two unconclusive chases, Marmite provided a bogie on which AI contact was secured at two miles. Closing through 'window' to 900 ft., a visual was obtained on an unusually bright exhaust of a target taking mild evasive action. The range was closed to between 50 and 100 ft., with the target at twelve o'clock, fifteen degrees, visual identification was made of an Fw 190. . . . The Balkan crosses on the fuselage were clearly visible at this range illuminated by the light of exhaust coming from the engine. Pulling up and dead astern, the night fighter opened fire at ranges varying from between 100 and 400 ft. After several bursts, strikes were observed on the German aircraft followed by a tremendous explosion producing a violent white-hot fire in the engine. The aircraft wobbled for a moment and then fell off to port. As the enemy aircraft fell, the pilot could no longer see the exhaust flames from the engine which had been very noticeable before the combat engagement. Owing to the cloud cover, he could not see the aircraft strike the ground, but Marmite advised that they were sure the kill was made."

Graham observed recently: "That was funny. Our gun sight was off and Bob [Bolinder] came up. We didn't use tracers because it gave our position away, and we came up behind him higher and nothing happened. We fired again. The guy couldn't have been looking for us. We were directly behind him and probably less than 100 yards away. Finally, Bob pulled the nose of our ship up, then fired. Then he pulled down and pulled up again as he fired, making an 'X.' We got him. He didn't burn as he went into the cloud cover; his prop was standing straight up.

"The 101st Airborne were cut off at Bastogne. They were pretty happy to see

The Creep *is parked next to* Plenty Peed Off *after returning from their night sortie against the Germans. Note the star on* Plenty's *nose wheel.* USAF

us; we took the air pressure off their necks. The weather became clear enough for the Germans to fly again. We shot down a number of them in that area. I bumped into a couple of the 101st troops when I was on rest leave in England. They wouldn't let me buy any drinks for a long time they were so grateful."

With this kill, Lieutenant Bolinder returned to base to rearm and refuel. With the noticeable increase of activity, all crews were put on alert. The next three crews that were sent up had ample contacts and many chases—a good bit of it being with low-flying aircraft—but no tangible results. In the early morning hours of December 17, Bolinder and Graham were in the air again. Within thirty minutes they had made AI contact and destroyed an Me 110. Shortly afterward they destroyed another enemy aircraft, this time an He 111.

In night-fighting, positive visual identification was mandatory to preclude the accidental damage or destruction of friendly aircraft, though this did occur in a number of cases. Bolinder made contact with yet a fourth aircraft on this night, but it looked too much like a Lockheed Lodestar. He was not able to pursue it and positively identify. Reports came back later on in the war that this was an Italian aircraft taking a number of top-ranking Nazis to Spain.

The weather became so severe by December 28 that it was necessary to cancel nearly all air operations on both sides. Germany's grand offensive had been stopped, mainly by Allied air power, and the Germans were beginning an orderly retreat. In the air, the night fighters scored seventeen enemy aircraft destroyed, one probable, and one damaged (17-1-1) during the offensive. The bad weather limited day operations of the 422nd's P-61s and A-20s. These aircraft did yeoman service in ground-attack operations that followed. The A-20s dropped nearly twelve tons of general purpose bombs and flew strafing missions as did the unit's P-61s, concluding the month with the claim of three locomotives destroyed, fifty-seven railroad cars damaged and eight motor transports destroyed or damaged.

The 422nd had been in combat for five months when the offensive began. During this time they had received only one replacement aircraft! All their aircraft had over 300 combat hours, which was beginning to show on both the aircraft and their radar sets. Serviceability of their war-weary aircraft was very low, and at times, the 422nd was able to operate with as few as four aircraft, each of these flying three or four missions in one night. They had lost five aircraft (three P-61s) and one crew during the Ardennes offensive. The major cause of these losses was weather. It was felt that if they had been equipped with the long-range external fuel tanks, as they had requested many times, these aircraft would not have been lost.

The 425th brought the war right into the German's back yard. One night the 425th's CO, Maj. Leon G. Lewis and his R/O, Lt. Karl E. "Souky" Soukikian, were flying near Strasbourg, France, when they spotted the head and tail lights of a convoy that snaked through the entire length of that Rhine city. Lewis had no more than started his dive toward the tail of the convoy than the sky was filled with flak. There wasn't anyplace to turn. The entire airplane was holed like a piece of Swiss cheese. Their radio equipment and electrical compass were knocked out. Lewis and Soukikian later reported: "Flying by gyro compass in the dark through turbulent, flak-filled air is much like jitterbugging with a nervous girl while wearing roller skates on ice." The 425th's CO gives Souky all the credit for finding their field that night—a mighty fine job of navigating.

The German high command realized that Allied air power was stopping Operation Greif (the Ardennes counteroffensive). In an attempt to regain the advantage, Operation Hermann was initiated. This was to be a massive air attack by the Luftwaffe against all Allied airfields on the Continent. The Germans were not able to initiate operations due to bad weather until New Year's Day, when they flew more than 800 sorties, most at low level. Though they destroyed nearly 150 Allied aircraft, it also proved to be quite disastrous to the Luftwaffe. This effort ended their last great offensive, and it was a question from here on out of the Allies attempting to turn the Germans' orderly retreat into a rout.

While flying a patrol in the Hamburg area, the 425th crew of Lt. Stan O. Wooley (pilot) and Lt. Robert W. Llovet (R/O) observed a train off in the distance. Being the skilled train-busters they were, they pointed their venomous spider plane at their prey and unleashed a deadly web of cannon fire. Right on the money, but it must have been an ammunition train. It seemed as if the train came up after them. Their plane was peppered in a dozen places by the flying debris; and to make matters worse, their radio gear was knocked out. Now the problem was to find their home base without their radio.

First they tried to find familiar landmarks to help them get their bearings. Then they aimed their nose for what they hoped was the right direction and poured on the coal. As they neared friendly lines they signaled SOS with their lights. But all this did was to bring on ground fire—enemy as well as friendly. They continued the flashing in hopes of convincing the friendly forces that they were not the enemy and needed help, but the friendly fire continued. At last Lieutenant Wooley figured out the problem: they had been flashing RPR, not SOS.

Finally, across the line and in not much worse shape, Wooley and Llovet hoped that some kind searchlights could be found and guide them in. No such luck. Doing the best they could—which was quite good under the circumstances—they managed to locate their own field. Still without a means of communication and in the dark of night, they couldn't tell which way to come in. The only thing was to take a chance on direction and hope for the best. It was the wrong way, and it wasn't long before they were aware of it. The crew of Lt. Alvin E. Anderson and Lt. John G. Smith were headed right for them. Somehow they managed not to hit anyone and got their ship down.

The Air War against Germany Winds Down

The air war in the MTO was winding down as 1945 began. In early January the Mosquito-equipped 416th NFS at Pisa, Italy, sent a detachment of their Mosquitos to Etain, France, to work along with the Ninth Air Force's 425th NFS. The 414th Night Fighter Squadron, based at Pontedera, Italy, had shortly before concluded its transition from Beaufighters to P-61s. In mid-January they had sent a detachment to Florennes, Belgium. Here they would gain further combat experience in their new aircraft while operating in support of the 422nd NFS.

The 425th made a deadly affair for their Axis enemies by using napalm bombs in conjunction with rockets on night intruder missions. The tactic was to first light up the targets with 165 gallon tanks filled with napalm and make a firing pass with their rockets. These missions prompted XIX Tactical Air Command to state, "Night intruder operations form an important and necessary complement to the daylight fighter-bomber activities, giving the enemy no rest."

In the European theater of operations, the invasion of Germany was just about a month away in February 1945. The emphasis on aerial operations was placed on crippling what remained of the German transportation system. The 425th Night Fighter Squadron of XIX TAC flew 117 sorties out of Etain, France, fifty-one of them being intruder missions in which napalm, 500 lb. general purpose bombs and 5 in. HVARs were used against rail and road traffic and associated installations.

Aerial combat was in a marked decline during the first quarter of 1945. For January, the 414th, 422nd and 425th each came through with one confirmed kill. The 414th's Belgium detachment was the only night fighter unit under Ninth Air Force control to come up with a victory during February. March operations were not much better.

Cpls. Arthur Wilitscher and Roy Challberg, ground crew with the 425th NFS, check the propeller of Sleepy Time Gal, *a P-61A-10, serial number 42-5576. Sept. 27, 1944, France. USAF*

The 422nd was credited with four confirmed and one damaged; the 425th scored one confirmed. The one bright spot for the night fighters was the addition of another team to the fraternal order of night fighter aces. It happened in the early morning hours of March 2 when the 422nd's crew of Lts. Herman Ernst and Edward Kopsel were flying just east of the Rhine River. Within about a twenty-minute period Ernst and Kopsel destroyed two Ju 87s and severely damaged an Me 110, making them the third AAF night fighter team and the second for the 422nd Night Fighter Squadron to attain the five-kill mark.

Besides their P-61s, the 425th began flying Douglas A-20s in the war against Axis ground forces. The Ninth's night fighter squadrons completed the month by dropping twenty-two tons of bombs, forty-eight 165 lb. napalm bombs, with the 425th firing eighty-four 5 in. HVARs. Because of total darkness in which the night fighters operated, all results could not be tallied: over thirty locomotives were either damaged or destroyed with nearly a hundred rail cars damaged, about the same score against motor transports, and unconfirmed damages against many fixed installations.

In the early morning hours of March 21, the 422nd scored its third and fourth kills for that month. On patrol that night was Capt. Raymond A. Anderson and 2nd Lt. Robert F. Graham as his R/O. They had been flying a defensive patrol of the First Army area west of the Rhine. The report of their encounter reads as follows:

"Their patrol period was more or less uneventful, and a few chases by Marmite control (GCI station) were lost due to a faulty weapon. At 0015 hours, while returning to base, Marmite informed them a bogey was approaching from the southeast (Coblenz area) at 8,500 ft. After several vectors from ground control, the airborne radar picked up this target at 1½ miles, taking violent evasive action in the form of 180 degree turns, dives, and climbs. AI contact was lost several times and regained with the help of Marmite. Finally, after three unsuccessful runs, AI contact was again obtained at 1½ miles. The bogey was still 'jinking' violently. This time range was closed to 1,200 ft. where Captain Anderson received a visual on twin

exhaust and tails, target travelling generally 270, altitude by now 3,500 ft., IAS 140-150. Finding it difficult to stay in position behind the target, Captain Anderson opened his cowl flaps to slow himself down. At 300 ft. range, target 30 degrees above, the bogey was identified as a Do 217-K2 by twin tails, tapered wings, and pencil shape fuselage. For some reason the bandit abandoned evasive action and was flying straight and level. Captain Anderson then dropped back dead astern and climbed slightly above the enemy aircraft. At 400 ft. range, fire was opened with one long burst, and the target immediately exploded and burst into flames, debris and fire trailing off. Turning and diving to port to avoid collision, Captain Anderson saw the bandit pass over his starboard wing, and Lieutenant Graham was able to distinguish the German crosses, saw one wing fall off and a parachute open. The target crashed into the ground and burned fiercely, combat terminating at 0045 hours."

For Lieutenant Graham this was the fifth kill that he assisted in, his previous four being with his regular pilot, Lt. Robert G. Bolinder, making Graham the AAF's first and only R/O participating in five kills with different pilots.

The 425th NFS team of Lts. Cletus T. Ormsby and Davis M. Howerton, Jr., made their sixth and final claim on Mar. 28, 1945. Unfortunately, Lieutenant Ormsby was killed on the mission. It was during the big push of the previous December that they got their first kills—a Do 217 on the twenty-fifth and then on the night of Dec. 30, 1944, they got a pair of Luftwaffe night fliers, a Ju 188 and an Me 110. On that fateful day of late March, they were in the process of shooting down a Ju 87 Stuka.

Just as the Ju 87 exploded and started down, their P-61 was rocked by a lethal dose of flak (there is some question as to which side's antiaircraft batteries it came from). Howerton could see that Ormsby had been killed (the 425th was the only squadron that modified their turretless P-61s by moving the R/O's equipment from the aft of the crew nacelle to the gunner station behind and above the pilot). Not aware of how seriously wounded he was, Howerton managed to get the hatch off and pull himself up and out. He egressed

from the crippled Widow successfully. As he floated down in his parachute he observed the plane in its death dive. He soon, unfortunately, landed in a tree.

In the dark he could not tell how far off the ground he was or the extent of his wounds (he had sustained shrapnel wounds in both thighs). Hearing German voices he decided to cut his parachute shroud lines and fall to the ground. The impact was too much, a broken bone came through his thigh. The voices he heard soon caught up to him; locals who had planned to bring about his early demise.

Fortunately, the Wehrmacht were in the area and took him into their custody. Howerton recalled that "the Wehrmacht picked me up and I went first to a German aid station then to a hospital where the damn' Jerrys proceeded to save my life! A crazy war."

Between late March and early May, the 422nd, along with the 414th's detachment, moved from their muddy quarters in Belgium onto German soil. Lt. Col. Churchill K. Wilcox, staff weather officer for the 422nd Night Fighter Squadron, remembered that move very well:

"We left our happy home in the mud of Belgium in March 1945 to go to the enemy country for the first time on the ground. Our first station in Germany was Euskirchen (Strassfeldt) near Bonn. We were there only a short time before the fast pace of events dictated a move far to the east, to Langensalza, now in the Russian zone—oops! I mean the 'German Democratic Republic,' otherwise known as East Germany. We inhabited a huge caserne or barracks which had been, until a short time before, one of the top training bases for the Luftwaffe. It was of great interest to us to learn that Langensalza had, in fact, been the principal training base for the German night fighters. There were several Ju 88s modified for night fighting. We inspected their radar and concluded that they were much more primitive than ours, at least from the standpoint of an R/O.

"The base was in fairly good repair overall, and we had some duties as occupying forces with the local populace. For example, I had occasion to use my German in connection with the enforcement of regulations sent down from Military Government on the turning in of all firearms and other types of weapons. I never saw such a collection of seventeenth century flintlocks, smooth-bore muskets, ancient shotguns and fowling pieces, and other completely useless items of weaponry. Many of which, I suppose, had been handed down from one generation to the next as heirlooms. It made no difference; we had to enforce the rules. I also had to explain to one middle-aged man why he could not enter a Luftwaffe warehouse full of warm, wool uniforms and lined boots to get something to keep himself warm. About all I could say to him was, 'Es ist streng vertoten,' and watch him walk sadly away. I felt absolutely no compunction at seeing the plight of German soldiers as prisoners of war, some of whom had killed my buddies; but to see a civilian shivering in the cold within a few feet of warm clothing which was going to be destroyed anyway was a little hard."

As the end was nearing, American forces made excursions into "forbidden" territory. The night fighters did their part in these unofficial operations.

Russ Glasser, 425th NFS commander, recalled: "We received another mission involving Col. Morrie Rose, and a trip into Germany that he took. The mission lasted for two days and two nights; we flew the night missions. After the mission was completed, I expected either to get busted or a compliment, at least in the Navy they usually sent you a signal, 'well done.' So for two days I sweated because I heard absolutely nothing. I didn't know what to do. Then one morning about ten o'clock the first sergeant woke me and said that there was a captain outside from General Patton's headquarters who wanted to see me. I knew then that I was on my way home in handcuffs. But when I got to the squadron office there was the captain and three 6x6 trucks. He said, 'Major, the first two trucks are loaded with beer; the third truck is loaded with whiskey. General Patton's compliments—have a party on him. Thanks!'"

An increase in Luftwaffe air transport activity enabled the 422nd NFS to end the last full month of the war with ten confirmed victories. The 414th's detachment, which remained with the 422nd until the latter moved to Langensalza, shot down four Luftwaffe planes, one of which was an Me 410.

On the night of Apr. 11, the 422nd showed the Luftwaffe what a crack night fighter outfit could do. One of the crews in the air during this time was Lt. Eugene D. Axtel with Lt. Creel H. Morrison as his R/O. They made AI contact with an aircraft flying at 600 ft. range and at an altitude of 1,000 ft. Positive identification was made of the aircraft, a Ju 52. It was an easy kill. A short time later Axtel and Morrison made a repeat performance destroying their second Ju 52 for the night, and brought Axtel's total confirmed victories to date to five destroyed and two damaged. He became the third pilot to reach acedom in the 422nd, and the fourth recognized by the AAF. Before the night was over the 422nd had successfully intercepted and destroyed seven more enemy aircraft, bringing the squadron's total for the night to seven Ju 52s and two Ju 88s. The following night, Apr. 13, 1945, the squadron got its tenth kill of the month and last claim for the war. Lt. Theodore I. Jones and his R/O, Lt. William G. Adams, successfully intercepted a bandit at 0303 hours. It was a Ju 52.

At 0001 hours on May 9, 1945, the unconditional surrender of all German forces became effective. The war in Europe was over. Another war, far to the west, was still being waged, however. Though the night fighters of the ETO were slated to go into combat against the Japanese, that war would end before the required movements could be accomplished.

Chapter 7

Tiger Country

When one thinks of the China-Burma-India (CBI) theater, and in particular the combat operations in China, Maj. Gen. Claire L. Chennault and his American Volunteer Group (AVG, or the Flying Tigers), who flew in defense of Burma and China prior to America's entry into the war, usually come to mind. In the scheme of things, it was quite late in the war before the AAF's night fighter arm entered the conflict in this part of the world.

Conflict and confrontation are usually accepted as part of war. In the CBI theater, it was much more. In China,

P–61s destined for either the 426th or 427th NFSs of the China-Burma-India theater wait on Army barges in the harbor of Calcutta, India. US Army

there was not *a* government, but a number of them: the Nationalist government of Chiang Kai-shek, the Communist under Mao Tse-tung, and the puppet government of the Japanese-controlled territories (not to mention the warlords who controlled smaller areas). There were also the usual squabbles within the Allied ranks. American and British cooperation had its usual rough spots. Chiang Kai-shek and Lt. Gen. Joseph "Vinegar Joe" W. Stilwell had quite a feud before Stilwell was replaced, and Maj. Gen. Claire Chennault of the Fourteenth Air Force and Maj. Gen. Curtis E. LeMay (commanding Twentieth Air Force's B-29s in the CBI) had to contend for the limited resources available. It was in this conflict that the night fighters were embroiled before they arrived.

General LeMay feared what the advancing Japanese war forces could do to his fledgling B-29 operations out of Chengtu, China. He had requested of Gen. Henry H. "Hap" Arnold, Army Air Forces commanding general, that night fighters be dispatched to protect this base from night attack. General Chennault felt that the night fighters would overburden his supply lines to such an extent that it would be impossible to supply them and reduce even further the operations of the other units under his command. Like everything else, fuel—the lifeblood of flying operations—had to be flown over the Hump from India. Chennault informed Arnold of his evaluation of the situation.

Soon Col. Winston W. Kratz was dispatched to China to bring about a solution. Colonel Kratz was the com-

manding officer of the 481st Night Fighter Operational Training Group, which developed the AAF's night fighter tactics and doctrine and trained its night fighter forces. He was a frequent emissary of Arnold's to overseas areas when night fighter operations or tactics were requested. On this mission, Kratz traveled with sealed orders—orders that were to be opened only if Chennault remained steadfast and refused to support the night fighter squadron designated to be assigned to the Fourteenth Air Force. Kratz later learned that because of the priority that the B-29 program held, Chennault was to be relieved per the sealed orders if he did not agree to the assignment. After much discussion, Chennault agreed with the need for this squadron and assured Kratz that somehow they would be supported logistically.

426th NFS

With their training as a unit completed, the 426th NFS packed their bags and left California's sunny San Joaquin Valley in mid-June 1944. Their first stop was Newport News, Virginia, where they boarded ship for a slow boat (no, not quite to China) to India. Aboard the USS *General A. E. Anderson* along with the night fighters were a number of WACs (Women's Army Corps), which diverted some attention away from the long sea voyage. Arriving on August 8, they boarded a train that took them to their next stop, Calcutta. Their destination, for a while at least, was Camp Kanchapara, about forty miles from Calcutta. They would have quite a bit of time on their hands, because it wasn't until late September that their Widows arrived by ship in Calcutta.

During this period, some of the ground echelon was sent to Sylhet, Bangladesh, on temporary duty with a combat cargo unit. When P-61s were unloaded on the Calcutta docks, these partially disassembled craft were transported to Barrackpore where they were reassembled by Air Service Command. Once checked out, the 426th NFS took possession of the planes and flew them to Madhaiganj Air Base. During the next couple of weeks, the planes would be rotated to Ondal, where Air Service Command modified them (one of the modifications being additional radio equipment).

P-61s being reassembled and checked out at the Air Service Command depot at Barrackpore, India. Much local labor was used at the depot. The weathered appearance of these aircraft was caused during the removal of the protective cosmolene coating that had been applied to protect them during sea transport. Northrop via Balzer

October 5 marked the start of the 426th's combat deployment; four aircraft were sent to Chengtu, China, to start operations. Guiding the four black birds was the squadron's commanding officer, Maj. William C. Hellriegel, flying a B-25H with other personnel and equipment. Their mission was night defense for the B-29s based in the Chengtu area. Arriving at the same time was the entire air echelon of twelve P-61s of the 427th Night Fighter Squadron led by their commanding officer, Lt. Col. James L. Michael, in a B-25C.

Col. Winston W. Kratz of the 481st NFOTG in California congratulates Capt. Robert R. Scott of the 426th NFS for scoring that unit's first victory. Scott, along with F/O Charles W. Phillips, his R/O, destroyed a Lily on the night of Oct. 29, 1944. Kratz was on a special mission in China at the time to persuade Gen. Claire Chennault that he had to support the night fighters. Reynolds

The insignia of the 426th NFS.

427th NFS

The 427th NFS arrival in the CBI had been somewhat circuitous. They had left their training base in California on July 12, a month after the 426th had departed. Their destination was Poltava, Russia. They were to be part of special missions code named Frantic. The plan was to establish fields and facilities in the Ukraine. The theory was that long-range bombing missions could be flown into Germany and other German-held territory and then, instead of a long return flight back to home bases, the bombers and escorting fighters would go on to the Russian bases.

Three bases were established in the Kiev areas—Poltava, Mirgorod and Piryatin. The first of these "shuttle" missions was flown by the Fifteenth Air Force on June 2, 1944, followed by an Eighth Air Force mission on June 21. The Eighth Air Force's mission was a very successful bombing mission. *But*, a German night attack created mass havoc and destroyed a major part of the bomber force on the ground. Though the Germans were not able to repeat this destruction by night, reevaluation of the requirement for this type of mission, and political problems, led to the cessation of Frantic after the Eighth Air Force had flown six missions.

The 427th NFS had split up into ground and air echelons in California. The air echelon flew their P-61s to the east coast of the United States where they and their aircraft were loaded on a Canadian and an American aircraft carrier. The ground echelon followed and went by troop ship. On August 8 the aircraft carriers arrived at Casablanca, French Morocco ("play it again, Sam" was probably in a number of minds),

A P-61 Black Widow night fighter in flight over Northern Burma. Having effectively discouraged all Japanese attempts to raid the area by night, the P-61s were equipped to carry 500 lb. bombs, and used as fighter-bombers to attack Japanese escape routes by day. They operated in the CBI theater under command of the Tenth AF. USAF

where they were unloaded. It was quite a sight to see twelve P-61s being towed through the streets of Casablanca by little Clark tugs, competing with the throngs of humanity that crowded its thoroughfares, along with camels, donkey-drawn carts and cars. Their destination was the air base at Gaza where the planes would be assembled and checked out.

On August 22 all was finished and the aircrews flew their planes to Cairo, Egypt. Here they found some unexpected news—their orders were changed and Poltava was scrubbed. They were to join the four Beaufighter-equipped night fighter squadrons of the Twelfth Air Force in the Mediterranean area. After about a week's stay in Cairo, the air echelon departed and arrived at the 19th Replacement Depot outside of Naples, Italy, where they joined up with the ground echelon for the first time since leaving the States. Their new assignment was to provide night air defense from Pomigliano, which started upon their arrival on September 3. Their stay was short, however; on September 20 they were given the orders to pack their bags again. This time their destination was the CBI.

Though they were in operation in the Naples area for less than three weeks, they were able to fly a number of missions and had contacts with German

reconnaissance aircraft from northern Italy. On one of these missions, a radar malfunction experienced just before firing range prevented possible destruction of the Widow's prey. On the other mission in which contact was accomplished, the attack was cut short when the Naples antiaircraft defenses tried to help and nearly shot down their first Black Widow. With the departure of the 427th NFS, the Mediterranean theater of operations would not have P-61s assigned again until late December, when the 414th NFS would trade their war-weary Beaufighters for Black Widows.

426th and 427th in Combat

Sterling cooperation was accomplished between the 426th and the 427th NFSs. The 426th, with only four operational Widows, needed additional aircraft for their Chengtu operations. A deal was struck between the COs of the two squadrons in which the 427th would give the 426th eight of its twelve aircraft in exchange for the 426th's aircraft at the depot at Karachi, Pakistan, where two were assembled and six were being assembled. At this time the 427th was assigned to Pandaveswar, India.

By the end of October 1944 the 426th NFS was at full strength at Chengtu, China. On October 27, a detachment of the 426th initiated operations out of

Kunming, China, where Fourteenth Air Force was headquartered. The first enemy aircraft destroyed by the P-61 in the CBI occurred on the night of October 29 (some reports show it as October 30) with Capt. Robert R. Scott, pilot, and F/O Charles W. Phillips manning the radar. They had been airborne for quite some time when GCI vectored them toward the enemy aircraft. The combat report states the following:

"GCI immediately gave me two vectors and altitude, enemy aircraft was forty miles away, I flew with throttle wide open and gentle in a climb from 5,000 ft. First AI contact 2½ to 3 miles away. A visual was made at 11,000 ft. altitude with the enemy aircraft approximately 1,000 ft. away, it was very hard to distinguish. The enemy aircraft was taking gentle turns and climbing a hundred twenty mph. The enemy aircraft came into my sight at 600 ft. and I fired at 500 ft. simultaneously with my fire enemy aircraft took hard, deep diving turn to left. A dogfight took place which lasted five minutes. . . . I don't know exactly what happened, I stalled a couple of times, we dived, climbed and turned hard in both directions. At about 4,000 ft. I came into position to fire again, still diving I got a burst of about 60 rounds per gun. I could see the bullets hitting the starboard wing and engine, a slight yellow flame came out of the underside of the starboard engine. Small flaming fragments blew off the enemy aircraft. I was close and pulled right for fear of enemy aircraft blowing up in front of me. My instinct was to get away, for my altitude was 3,000 ft. I started to orbit and climb during which time I checked the ground but could see no fire. Upon returning to base I found there was a large nick in my propeller. My radar observer had me in ideal position the first time I opened fire."

November was a very busy month for the CBI's two night fighter squadrons. A detachment of three P-61s and support personnel left the main body of the 427th NFS in India and went to Myitkyina South, in Burma, coming under the control of Tenth Air Force. On the night of November 21 there was much aerial activity. Five P-61s were alerted for patrol duty; among the crews were that of Capt. Robert R. Scott and F/O Charles W. Phillips, and that of Capt. John J. Wilfong and 2nd Lt. Glenn

The 427th's P-61s had an additional piece of equipment atop the crew nacelle—an automatic direction finder (ADF). Because of its shape it was referred to as a football. This

P-61A-10-NO, serial number 42-39349, was photographed at Myitkyina, Burma, January 1945. K. Sumney

E. Ashley. During their encounters, Scott and Phillips were credited with a "damaged," while Wilfong and Ashley were credited with their first enemy aircraft destroyed.

After takeoff, Wilfong was vectored by GCI to 6,000 ft. where the enemy aircraft was. Wilfong was going too fast and overshot. GCI got him back on course and brought him to within four miles of the target. At this time, Lieutenant Ashley picked up the enemy craft on his radar. The enemy became aware that he was being pursued and began taking mild evasive action. The night fighter climbed to 14,000 ft. and made visual contact of his target—600 ft. ahead. A short burst of about forty rounds, and the enemy aircraft exploded.

On November 28 another contingent of the 427th NFS arrived at Myitkyina, North this time. More of the squadron arrived during December—basically by truck over the Ledo Road—from their headquarters in India to prepare Myitkyina North as the squadron's new headquarters (where they would remain well into May 1945). During December, the 427th's small detachment of three P-61s at Myitkyina South saw all there was of aerial "action." They participated in seventeen combat missions. Of these, twelve proved to be friendly aircraft with inoperable or without identification, friend or foe (IFF). Three were patrols ordered by higher headquarters, and two were enemy aircraft (none were destroyed).

On December 25 a detachment of the 427th NFS arrived at Kunming, China, relieving the 426th's detachment. All but one crew returned to their main base at Chengtu. Capt. John Pemberton, pilot, along with his R/O, Lieutenant Cliby, and Staff Sergeant Thomas flew to India to pick up the first P-61B in the theater.

A detachment of the 426th NFS was based at Guskhara, India, in January 1945, and would be there into August. Crews would also be spending short periods of detached service at Kunming and Hsian, China, on a regular basis.

Two more enemy aircraft were destroyed by the 426th's P-61s in January, both in the Laohokow area. The first of these occurred on January 27, when Capt. Carl J. Absmeier and his R/O, Lt. James R. Smith, were on patrol and GCI got a contact at the twenty-four-mile

range. Smith picked up the target at four miles and brought Absmeier to within 1,500 ft. where visual identification was made. At 200 to 300 ft. Absmeier fired, setting the enemy aircraft on fire. Oil from the burning plane smeared the P-61's windshield and prevented visual contact with another plane that Smith had picked up on his scope. Three nights later, this same team was airborne when GCI vectored them to a target. They closed in and at 700 ft. a visual was made. Absmeier closed to 500 ft. on the Lily bomber and started firing. The bomber started to burn and exploded in the air.

Action was not quite the same for the 427th NFS. The bulk of the squadron was now in Burma. During January, they flew patrols over Myitkyina and Bhamo and twelve local tactical interceptions. No enemy aircraft was encountered. Unfortunately for the 427th, one of those misfortunes of war occurred. On January 22 one of its aircraft in the China detachment operating out of Suichwan shot down a US C-87 with a crew of nine. The C-87 was in a prohibited area and made no radio calls, which led to the conclusion that it was hostile.

February 1945 saw the last aerial victory for the P-61 in the CBI. On February 8 the 426th's 1st Lt. Harry W. Heise, and R/O F/O Robert C. Brock were on patrol in the Laohokow area when GCI vectored them to a plane that had just dropped its bombs. Brock made radar contact and the chase was on. For fifteen to twenty minutes they chased the enemy, going through several hard turns. Finally, visual contact was made; they were 700 ft. from the target. As he closed to 350 ft., Heise opened fire; the Lily bomber exploded.

Night Intruder Missions

From this point on, Japanese night flying nearly ceased. More and more, the two night fighter squadrons were flying night intruder missions. The 426th started staging out of Ankang, Liangshan, and Sian, China, from which they attacked communication, motor transport and rail lines. The 427th NFS modified their aircraft to carry a three-tube bazooka-type rocket launcher under

The 426th NFS's first operational base in China was at Chengtu, from which they were to protect the B-29 Superforts from night raiders. With the B-29s going to the central Pacific, and diminishing Japanese night activity, they spent most of their time in the role of night intruder and ground attack during daylight hours.

Maj. W. C. Hellriegel stands in the cockpit of his P–61, Tommie. Hellriegel flew with the 426th as they fought against the Japanese *forces in China during 1944 and 1945.* Bob Brendel

each wing. With their rocket-carrying Widows, they operated against Japanese forces from their bases at Myitkyina in Burma as well as Kunming in China.

The 427th NFS intruder missions started on February 22 with a sweep of the road network south of Lashio, Burma. The squadrom flew seven night intruder sorties that month. In mid-March, day and night offensive reconnaissance missions covering Pangkeyhtu/Loi-lem/Ho-pong/Namsang road network. Thirty-three day and night patrols were accomplished that month. Missions staged out of Kunming and Chihkiang were curtailed in April because of a shortage of fuel. 427th headquarters moved from Burma to Kisselbarri, near Dinjan, India, in late May. The detachment at Kunming remained there, operating elements from Chihkiang, Chengkung and Nanning until the war's end. Activity increased in July, with the squadron claiming 155 sampans destroyed and fifty-two damaged in addition to numerous warehouses, barges, trains and trucks destroyed. Besides flying day and night intruder sorties, two special medical supply airdrop sorties were flown in a BT–13A aircraft.

The 426th's activities were of the same type—strafing and bombing ground targets. While flying one of these missions on July 26, the team of Captain Wilfong and Lieutenant Ashley were hit by antiaircraft fire in one engine. They were able to nurse their wounded craft back across friendly lines and bail out. They made it back to Schwanliu on August 10! As it turned out, this was just in time.

On Aug. 13, 1945, the 427th was ordered to move to Liuchow, China. The air echelon flew there immediately while the ground echelon began the movement by road convoy. With the war over, the air echelon was ordered to fly to Yangkai, China, to turn in their aircraft for pickling and start processing home. The ground echelon's convoy was stopped at Ledo and turned around. About a month later the 426th returned to India, where some of the squadron left from Karachi and others from Calcutta for their return voyage home.

Chapter 8

Navy Widow

Navy interest in the P-61 had been more than casual from the start. When production was first being planned, the Navy had requested that it be so developed that their requirements could be met. Unfortunately this proved to be impractical, because Northrop Aircraft, manufacturer of the P-61, was experiencing difficulty in its development. In the summer of 1942, the US Navy again indicated their desire to obtain 200 of these craft for delivery in 1943. Following up on the Navy's overture, AAF Materiel Command issued instructions in early August to have a study made of Northrop's production with a view to increasing production to meet this added requirement. As brought out in earlier chapters, P-61 production had slipped to the point where Army Air Forces' requirements were not being met.

Interest in the Black Widow did not wane with time. Apparently, in about December 1943 the Navy Department approached the AAF again, this time for a small number of planes for test and experimental purposes. On Jan. 4, 1944, the AAF informed them that they should keep such requests for P-61s to an absolute minimum due to urgent AAF requirements in the combat theaters. Though this seemed to be a go-ahead for the procurement of a number of Widows by the Department of the Navy, there is no evidence that it took place. There is the possibility, however, that a number of Army 61s could have been borrowed.

Marines Fly the P-61

Not only night fighter aircraft but also training for the night-fighting Marines was being sought after in early 1944. In March of that year, Marine Lt. Col. M. A. Severson and six enlisted R/Os arrived in England. Attached to the USAAF's Ninth Air Force, they underwent night fighter training at the Royal Air Force's Cranfield Night Fighter Operational Training School. Five more pilots joined Severson a month later.

To gain firsthand knowledge of the P-61 under combat conditions, Severson was attached to the USAAF's 425th NFS at Scorton, England, where he was checked out. Once qualified, he went across the channel where he joined up with the USAAF's 422nd NFS at Cherbourg, France. During July and August 1944, Severson flew twenty combat missions with the 422nd from their Cherbourg and Chateaudun fields. In September he returned stateside, from whence he went to the Pacific to fly F4U Corsairs (the Marine Black Widow program was cancelled by this time).

Vice Adm. John S. McCain, Deputy Chief of Naval Operations (Air) wrote Gen. Hap Arnold in March 1944 concerning his desire to obtain P-61s to be used by Marine night fighter squadrons; it was to replace PV-1s, F4Us and F6Fs then in squadron use. Apparently, Admiral McCain was quite aware of Northrop's production capability, AAF requirements and that the present production rate could be increased beyond AAF requirements. The Navy could take up to twenty-five planes per month. General Arnold replied on March 28 that the matter would be investigated. By the end of the month an agreement was reached for an allocation of seventy-five aircraft to the Marines between July and December 1944. This news was not broken to the public until June 7, 1944,

when the *Northrop News*, house organ for Northrop Aircraft Co., announced in bold headlines, "Marines to Fly P-61." Also in June, Marine P-61 allocations were increased to ninety for 1944 and 150 for 1945.

An Army Air Forces Technical Training Unit had been established at the Northrop factory to train AAF technical personnel. On May 24, 1944, they were informed of the new Marine order and that they would be soon receiving their first cadre; a total of seventy-five Marines were scheduled. First Lt. William D. Bruckett arrived with the first contingent of eight enlisted Marines on June 15; the plan called for groups of eight enlisted men to arrive per week for seven weeks, and the remaining eleven men on the eighth week. It was about this same time that Marine night fighter squadron VMF(N)-531 flying Lockheed PVs in the Pacific was notified that it was scheduled to return to the United States to be reequipped with the P-61.

On July 10, 1944, the Office of the Chief of Naval Operations requested that the Navy P-61 allocations be cancelled. The seven reasons stated in their request all pointed to their preference for the Grumman F7F Tigercat over the P-61 (an aircraft that would not enter their inventory as a night fighter until October 1944 and would not see combat). At this time only thirty-two Marine mechanics had completed their training at Northrop, and VMF(N)-531, which was sent back to the States for the purpose of reequipping with the Widow, was deactivated.

It is somewhat ironic that the Marines would finally obtain P-61s, not to fly combat in, but to train in to prepare

The US Navy was interested in the P–61 from the beginning. As early as the summer of 1942 they started pressuring the Air Corps for a share of production. By mid–1944 they had their way, and the Marine Corps was to replace some of their PV–1 and other night fighter squadrons with the Widow. A training program was established at the Northrop plant to train Marine aircraft mechanics, as shown in this photo, in the care and feeding of the Widow. Northrop

for flying the F7F Tigercat. Under the command of Lt. Col. Homer G. Hutchinson, USMC, the Marine Night Fighter Operational Training Detachment was established at Vero Beach, Florida. A number of the men in the training organization had undergone earlier training in the P-61 at the Northrop factory or were part of the detachment under Lieutenant Colonel Severson in England. The mission of these Florida night fighters was to train operational crews in the F7F-3N.

In September 1945 twelve P-61Bs, a mix of P-61B-10s, 15s and 20s were obtained from the AAF. These aircraft were described as "aircraft in excess of Army requirements," and were transferred to the Department of the Navy at no expense. All but one of these aircraft came from the AAF's night fighter training organization at Hammer Field in California.

P-61 Becomes the F2T-1

The training syllabus at Vero Beach took sixteen weeks during which both pilot and R/O, individually and, during the last six weeks, as a team partook in many hours of ground training and airborne work in SNBs, F7F-2Ns, F7F-3Ns and F2T-1s. The SNBs and F7F-2Ns were equipped with APS-6 AI radar while the F7F-3Ns and F2T-1s carried SCR-720 equipment. Roominess in the R/Os compartment in the Widow enabled an instructor to ride with the R/O prior to turning the pilot and R/O team loose in the operational F7F-3N.

Though they had only twelve, the Marines had to change the Army's P-61 designation. But what to call it? Following the then-current designation scheme as prescribed by regulation, they came up with FT-1; *F* for fighter, *T* being the Northrop Aircraft Co. designator, and this being, so they believed, the first Northrop fighter in Navy/Marines inventory. This designation was carried for some time before it was discovered that FT-1 had already been used for a craft. So it was back to the drawing boards. The designation of F2T-1 was agreed upon and was officially accepted by the Department of the Navy.

The Black Widow's use in Florida was short-lived. In March 1946 one was destroyed at Jacksonville, Florida, for reasons that are not too clear. By April the training program was being phased out at Vero Beach and the weary 61s were starting to be ferried to MCAS (Marine Corps Air Station) Cherry Point, North Carolina, where they were to await further disposition. Operations ceased on May 1, and on that same date the last F2T took off from that field. But it didn't get too far. The pilot retracted the gear too soon and not having sufficient air speed, the big black bird settled back down on the runway. With a grinding crunch the plane came to a rest and was declared a total loss. With only minor injuries, the red-faced pilot left his crunched bird.

Four of the remaining F2Ts were assigned to the headquarters' squadron of Marine Air Group 53 at Cherry Point, and the remaining six were sent west to El Toro MCAS in Santa Ana, California, where they were put in storage. The four MAG53 aircraft were transferred to Miramar MCAS, San Diego, California, where they served in a support role. Their useful life ended in March 1947 when they were put in the Miramar pool (unassigned). By the end of June, all had been stricken (removed from inventory). The El Toro birds, though not put back into flying status, remained a little long-

#39, Cal-Donia is one of the "rare twelve," an F2T-1 used as a radar operator trainer in the Marine Corps. With ample available space in the R/O station, the P-61 allowed a trainer to ride with the trainee—providing the best training situation. Marine Corps

er. It wasn't until August 31, 1947, that the last two of these planes were officially stricken.

Special Purpose P-61s

There were a number of "special purpose" P-61s used by the Department of the Navy. At its Patuxent River test

facility in Maryland, the Radio Test Division used P-61B-1, serial number 42-39458, in a number of tests. At another Navy test base, this time Mustin Field, Pennsylvania, P-61A-10, serial number 42-39395, was subjected to a test that the Navy put most AAF fighters through—a catapult test. The standard

procedure was to carry out about fifty catapult launches to qualify an aircraft for shipboard launches. Most of the Widow work was accomplished with Navy Lt. Robert M. Elder at the controls.

In 1946 the Navy let a contract with the Glenn L. Martin Company to produce a rocket airframe to house an experimental Marquardt Co. ramjet engine. Designated PTV-N-2U Gorgon IV, this rocket was strictly of the experimental category. The Marquardt Co. was a relatively new concern. It was organized by a number of former Northrop engineers and Roy E. Marquardt, who at the time was director of Aeronautical Research at the University of Southern California. Their sole purpose was the research and production of ramjet engines. Powering the Gorgon IV was their third engine model designated C-20.85C.

Some means are required to bring a ramjet-powered vehicle to the necessary speed for the ramjet engine to function. There are a number of ways by which this can be accomplished. Either supplemental powerplants on the ramjet-equipped vehicle can be used, or the ramjet vehicle can be carried to altitude and speed by another vehicle, sometimes referred to as a mother ship. Here the Black Widow enters the picture. In this instance, two P-61Cs (serial numbers 43-8336 and 43-8347) were borrowed from the Air Force and used on the Gorgon missile project. Flight operations were initiated at Martin Field outside of Baltimore, Maryland, but were shortly moved to the Naval Air Missile Test Center at Point Mugu in southern California.

In its role as mother ship, the Widow carried one Gorgon under each wing. A speed of Mach 0.5 was required before ramjet flight could be obtained. This required the P-61 to go into a slight dive. The first Gorgon was released from a Widow's wing on Nov. 14, 1947, while flying at 10,000 ft. Further tests would range in altitude from sea level up to 30,000 ft. A later phase of the test program was carried out by Navy experimental squadron VX-2 based at the Naval Aviation Ordnance Test Station at Chincoteague, Virginia. The F-61's involvement ended in 1948 with the return of the two aircraft to the USAF, and their subsequent transfer to the boneyards soon afterward.

This P-61, serial number 43-8336, was used as the mother ship in testing the PTV-N-2U Gorgon IV missile. With one Gorgon under each wing the Widow would reach speeds of *Mach 0.5 by going into a slight dive. This was the required speed for ramjet flight to be obtained.* Martin

This photo was taken seconds after the release of the Gorgon IV missile from the P-61C mother ship. The first of these missiles *was released from a Widow's wing on Nov. 14, 1947.* Martin

Chapter 9

Supercharged Widow

From the very beginning, performance was an important element in the development of a night fighter. The US Army Air Corps Military Characteristics of Aircraft-Pursuit, Night Interceptor of Jan. 9, 1941 (which came about after negotiations with Northrop Aircraft had started) called for maximum speed of 450 mph desired and 375 minimum at designed altitude. Jack Northrop had predicted 388 mph at 21,000 ft. for his dream-child night fighter.

A number of engineers at Northrop wanted to put turbosuperchargers on the P-61 in the early days, but pressures from the Air Corps prevailed against this. It is ironic that the AAF Board in Florida and the Washington "pencil pushers" did more yelling about the craft's performance than the ones who flew it. Of these negativists, a Wright Field colonel stated concerning their attitude toward the Widow, "They don't do much toward fighting the war; but when you move into a new island out there in the Pacific, you need them."

XP-61C

Aircraft, among other things, tend to take large advances in technology and performance under wartime conditions. The 1940 P-61 night fighter did need greater speed and altitude. By mid-1943, enough flight-test data from the P-61 program had been gathered and, when compared with enemy aircraft performance data from Europe and the Pacific, both the AAF and Northrop agreed that a higher performance P-61 was needed. Air Technical Service Command at Wright Field received word from AAF Headquarters on Nov. 11,

1943, to go ahead with such a project. The aircraft was to be the XP-61C.

The XP-61C was basically a standard Widow with improved engines. An R-2800-C engine was to replace the R-2800-B used in the earlier planes. Whether it was to be a two-stage, two-speed as were the earlier B model engines, or single-stage, and whether they were to have turbosupercharging or not, were all being considered. By early December 1943, the Fighter Project Office at Wright Field, in concert with Northrop Aircraft, decided that the two-stage engine installation would require a lot of redesign to be practical; so the single-stage C model engine was selected and turbosupercharging was to be uti-

The question of whether or not to use turbosuperchargers on the P-61 was part of early planning discussions. Because one of the principal requirements for the Widow was maximum loiter time, they were decided against because they increased fuel con-sumption. When designing the P-61s to be used for reconnaissance missions, speed became an essential component. Thus this turbosupercharged R-2800 was incorporated on the C and D models.

lized. Performance predictions at this time called for 430 mph at 30,000 ft.

Priorities at this time seem to have a detrimental effect on the P-61's development. In a memo from Wright Field to Washington in December, they stated that they would go "no further [on the XP-61C project] until instructed to do so." Instructions were not issued until mid-January 1944 for the incorporation of turbosupercharged single-stage, single-speed R-2800-C engines in one P-61. At Northrop Aircraft all shop space was being used at full capacity, and the Flying Wing project was consuming the engineering staff. Goodyear Aircraft at Akron, Ohio, which was doing a good bit of subassembly work for Northrop on the Black Widow, was selected to do the modification work. Basic engineering was accomplished by Northrop engineers; Goodyear engineers spent a good bit of time at the Northrop plant during the early stages and did the finishing work back at Akron.

The R-2800-77 engines with General Electric CH-5 turbosuperchargers were to power this aircraft. Unfortunately, other, higher-priority AAF aircraft had caused such a demand for this powerplant that none were to be available in the foreseen future. In their stead, the Navy R-2800-14W was to be used. In actuality, there were only minor differences between the two engines. Arrangements were made in January 1944 to obtain these engines.

In mid-February, a P-61A-5 was selected for this program. As a safety measure, Northrop suggested to the AAF that a second aircraft also be modified as a back-up should something happen to the first during flight testing. Permission was received later that same month. By this time the P-61A-10 variants were being manufactured, so the second aircraft selected for this test program was of this series. The mock-up was completed in early March, but it was decided to put off the formal mock-up inspection until early May. This was brought about because of changes required to improve serviceability of the plane, and it was decided to hold the inspection at the Goodyear plant.

XP-61D

By late April 1944 a number of changes had occurred. The powerplants to be used were now to be the R-2800-57. Then, on April 27, the Engineering Division at Wright Field ordered that the designation of the experimental aircraft be changed from XP-61C to XP-61D to prevent any confusion with the production C model. Unlike the A models in production, the XP-61D was to be modified to carry four wing pylons for external fuel tanks—a feature some B models and all C models would incorporate.

One feature that the production C would have, and not the experimental Ds, was dive or fighter brakes. This feature was recommended at the time of the XP-61 689 Engineering Inspection back in December 1942. Northrop had the third P-61A-1 (serial number 42-5487) loaned to them for the purpose of modifying it in such a manner. It was originally hoped that this feature could be incorporated in the production line with the 201st aircraft.

Technical and labor problems plagued the project during most of mid-year 1944. Goodyear found that it was impossible to meet the early delivery dates originally agreed to because of the redesign work required to meet the maintenance improvements. It also experienced extreme difficulty with the design and construction of the engine mounts. Manpower was also impeding progress; the draft was taking its toll of engineering and shop personnel. In addition, it seemed that very little assistance was being obtained from Northrop. Wright Field was experiencing this as well on all P-61 related work. Col. Mark E. Bradley, Jr., chief of the Fighter

Because of the workload at Northrop, the modification on the two P-61As to take the new engines was contracted out to Goodyear Aircraft at Akron, Ohio. Both of the XP-61Ds were scrapped at the end of their flight-test program. Pratt & Whitney

Branch, remarked during this period that ". . . we haven't been able to get much of anything done by Northrop because of so much priority on the B-35's."

The XP-61D was finally ready for the AAF inspector in November. First engine runs occurred on November 18, and the first flight came a few days later. Only minor difficulties were encountered during the preliminary flights, most of the problems were a result of General Electric's turbo regulator. One forced landing came about as a result of an oil line failure, but no damage was sustained.

The 689 Engineering Inspection was conducted on the second XP-61D during December 12 and 13. No major changes were requested. Several more suggestions were made to ease maintenance. Northrop agreed to incorporate these in the P-61C production aircraft.

Shortly after the 689 Inspection, propeller vibration tests were conducted on the first D model. One engine was equipped with A.O. Smith SPA-9 blades, and the other with Curtiss 836 blades. These tests took longer than planned due to test equipment problems, field conditions at Goodyear and bad weath-

P-61C fighter brake details. Northrop

The P-61C was equipped with fighter brakes to provide a means of preventing a pilot from overshooting his target when making *an intercept. During a maximum performance dive near Hawthorne, California, test pilot Max Stanley activated the fighter* *brakes and the huge aircraft seemed to stop in mid-air, leaving a lasting impression on Stanley.* Northrop

For added fuel capacity the P–61C was equipped with four underwing pylons, on which it could carry four 310 gallon drop tanks.

Flying chase to the YB–35 Flying Wing, serial number 42–13603, is the P–61C–1–NO Black Widow, serial number 43–8322. The Flying Wing was Jack Northrop's vision of the future. These two aircraft show the advanced technology and design prevalent in aircraft designed by Northrop, a tradition continued to include the current B–2 Stealth Bomber. Northrop

er. The Smith propellers provided the better performance. Once these tests were completed, both planes were flown to Northrop Field in California.

Flight Testing the C and D Models

At Northrop, the planes were to complete the final phase of testing and then were to be used for developmental work in conjunction with the production C model. Unfortunately, severe engine problems were encountered. Repeated engine failures made it impossible for the AAF to get good performance figures. But experience gained in fixing these problems did help in improving the engine design for the production planes. The improvements called for increased piston clearance, ring clearance and the addition of oil jets. Difficulties were also being had with the turbo exit. The exit allowed hot exhaust gas to flow along the bottom of the engine nacelle and tail boom, heating the structure above allowable limits.

AAF flight testing had begun shortly after the planes arrived at Northrop. When the engine failure problems were encountered, it was decided that the cooling tests were of greater importance. With the limited data that the AAF was able to obtain, they felt that had the airplane been in A-1 shape, it would have nearly met all of the performance guarantees.

Following the exhaust gas problem, tests were made to determine the optimal angle for the turbo exit, down and to the side, to prevent this problem. Soon after, R-2800-77 engines were installed. Further cooling tests showed the cooling now to be acceptable, though on the marginal side.

The flight-test program for the D models was completed by the fall of 1945. At that time both aircraft were in severe disrepair. It was estimated that considerable funds would have to be expended to bring these aircraft into acceptable condition to take part in further Army Air Forces flight tests. The P-61C had been in production for some time and a number had already been accepted, so the Ds were placed in Class 01-Z (scrapped or used in non-flying programs). The first XP-61D was scrapped on Sept. 11, 1945, and the second went in April 1946.

P-61C-1

Production of the P-61C-1 began in early 1945, with the first aircraft being accepted in July. Northrop and the Army Air Forces had been planning on a C model aircraft from the time that contract W535 ac-29319 calling for "207 Model P-61 airplanes" was approved in September 1943. Aircraft serial numbers 43-8231 through 43-8437 were assigned by the AAF to these 207 planes. The number of these aircraft that were to be produced as P-61C-1s changed with time. September 1943 AAF documents called out for 127 to be B models, and eighty to be C models. In September 1944 the P-61C-1 requirements were reduced to sixty-seven. The September 1945 document issue split the 207 aircraft into orders for six P-61B-25s, eighty-four P-61B-20s and ninety-eight P-61C-1s. Nineteen aircraft were cancelled from the contract.

The forty-first, and last, P-61C-1 was accepted on Jan. 28, 1946; at least thirteen completed aircraft were scrapped and never recorded on AAF records. Northrop documents show an additional 400 P-61Cs, with 1945 serial numbers, to have been on order. This is corroborated by Air Force documents

Congratulations from the AAF on Northrop's delivery of the 700th Black Widow (a P-61C). Those identified, from the left (standing) are Ted Coleman, vice president, sales; Dick Rinalde, production test pilot; Moye Stephens, corporate secretary and chief test pilot; Jack Northrop, president and chief of design; and Gage Irving (reading the document), vice president and assistant general manager. Northrop

which indicate that P-61C-5 and 10 block variants were at least in the planning stages.

The turbosupercharged powerplant with the A.O. Smith wide chord blades and fighter brakes differentiated the C Widow from its B model predecessor. Aircraft size and electronics were the same as the B model. Though this aircraft did achieve greater speed and altitude—the combat pilots who flew it felt that the increase in weight made it a lot less maneuverable—it was being quickly outclassed by the new jet aircraft. Even before the C model came off the Northrop production lines, thought was being given to the P-82 and P-83 as interim replacements prior to the fielding of the Curtiss-Wright P-87.

The operational use of the P-61C was mainly in the test and research fields. The closest thing to serving in an operational squadron was when twelve were sent to McChord Field, Washington, in November 1945. It is unclear as to the purpose of this deployment, as there was no night fighter squadron stationed there at that time. Within five months, all but two were transferred to Air Materiel Command and scattered across the country. It was with AMC that a majority of these aircraft saw duty, the most noted duty being on the Thunderstorm Project. Others served with NACA (National Advisory Committee for Aeronautics), were loaned to the US Navy, and a number of the aircraft were on loan to Northrop. By the end of March 1949, all remaining C aircraft were ordered into reclamation status (scrapped). Two of these planes went onto the civilian market, and two others went into museums.

Chapter 10

New Concepts

Consideration of the Black Widow as a bomber escort fighter was being discussed between Northrop Aircraft and the AAF even before the first production aircraft had been accepted. The

The first XP–61E on a test flight over the mountains. Balzer

cause for a P-61 long-range bomber escort was furthered by Northrop's John Myers during his Black Widow introduction tour in the Southwest Pacific Area during the summer of 1944. During conversations with V Fighter Command's chief, Brig. Gen. Paul B. Wurtsmith, and his chief of staff, Col. James O. Guthrie, it was realized that their requirements for

such an aircraft seemed to mesh with the bomber escort P-61 that Northrop had in the planning stages. At Fifth Air Force headquarters in Australia, Myers later had similar dialog with Lt. Gen. George C. Kenney.

When Myers came back to the States that fall, he took the P-61 bomber escort case to Wright Field. There he got the ear

The first XP–61E glides into the air as it takes off from Northrop Field near Hawthorne, California. The first flight of the modified P–61–B–10, serial number 42- *39549, occurred on Jan. 3, 1945, with Northrop test pilot L. A. "Slim" Parrett at the controls. Northrop*

of Col. Mark E. Bradley who was chief of the Fighter Branch. Bradley, convinced of the proposal's worth and Myers' sincerity, telephoned Col. J. F. Phillips, chief, Materiel Division, at Headquarters Army Air Forces, and got his support in the matter. With Phillips' support, Myers met with the Operations, Commitments, and Requirements, (OC&R) people on October 2.

XP-61E

It is of interest that Brig. Gen. Mervin E. Gross, chief of the Requirements Division, OC&R, prepared a memorandum for Maj. Gen. H. A. Craig, assistant chief of Air Staff (OC&R), in which he recommended that "the P-61 be considered only as a night fighter and that no effort be made to make a long-range day fighter out of this aircraft." As to General Kenney's support for the P-61 as an escort fighter, General Gross stated that it was based on the plane having C model engines with turbosuperchargers, additional fuel, turret and additional fixed guns. It also should be noted that earlier in that same year, January 1944, the AAF had let a contract to North American Aviation for the XP-82 (the production B model contract came a few months later), which was to fill the long-range bomber escort role.

For whatever reasons, contract W33-038 ac-2407 (the XP-61D contract) had a supplemental agreement issued against it calling for the development of two XP-61E airplanes. This route was chosen in order to expedite procurement of the aircraft. In October 1944, two P-61B-10s were accepted at the Northrop plant with the instructions that they were to be converted at the factory into XP-61Es. Number 1 XP-61E (serial number 42-39549) was completed in January 1945, and Number 2 (serial number 42-39557) was completed that March.

The conversion of the two B models into the E variant centered totally around the crew nacelle. All structures were removed from nacelle Station 33 forward, those from about Station 322 aft and everything from the top of the crew nacelle down to the waterline running in the plane parallel with the top of the wing structure. In place of the radar in the forward section were four .50 caliber machine guns with 300 rounds

This view from above the first XP-61E shows the modified cockpit with a bubble canopy. Weighing in at about 22,000 lb., this craft attained speeds somewhat greater than 370 *mph. With four 310 gallon auxiliary fuel tanks slung under its wings, it could attain ranges of over 4,000 miles.* Balzer

XP–61E, serial number 42–39549, in flight over the ocean. Balzer

each. Fuel tanks added to the crew nacelle provided an additional 518 gallons, plus the 640 in the internal wing tanks gave a total of 1,158 gallons of internal fuel. To provide an easy way to get into the cockpit, a ladder, which was an integral part of the fuselage side, was installed in the left side of the extreme aft section of the crew nacelle.

Though the equipment and general configuration of the two E aircraft were identical, there were two distinct differences. The bubble canopy on the first aircraft was hinged on the left side and swung to the left when opened. The canopy on the second plane rolled aft when opened. A second distinguishing feature

was the arrangement of the four .50 caliber machine guns in the two aircrafts' noses. Those in the first plane were in a box arrangement, when viewed from the front. The second airplane's were laid out more along a horizontal plane.

Very little data was gathered from the second aircraft, for it had been flying only about a month when a "hot" AAF pilot prematurely retracted the gear on a maximum performance takeoff, turning it into a pile of scrap. The Number 1 plane, however, showed the E model to have a distinct performance advantage over the P-61 night fighter variants, but it was not up to the performance stan-

dards of the latest fighters then entering both Allied and Axis air forces. The much greater calculated performance figures for the P-82, which wouldn't fly until June of 1946, probably sealed the fate of the project.

XF-15

Another project, that of a long-range reconnaissance aircraft, had been suggested for the P-61 at about the same time as the long-range escort proposition. Here, the performance of the streamlined E model was adequate. With less than six months' flying time, the Number 1 XP-61E went into the Northrop modification shop for a nose job. The transition from fighter to photo

This January 1945 photo of the second XP-61E being modified at Northrop gives a good idea of the "scalping job" that was performed. As can be seen, the original P-61B had its crew nacelle sliced off at the top of the wing. Further, the radar nose and R/O's compartment were removed. Balzer

recon was a matter of replacing the gun nose with one holding an assortment of aerial cameras. There also was a slight weight savings as the 20 mm cannons were removed and the gunports were covered over. The first flight of the XP-61E-turned-XF-15 came on July 3, 1945, with Northrop test pilot L. A. "Slim" Parrett at the controls.

F-15 Reporter

Even before the first flight of the XF-15, the OC&R people at AAF Headquarters had determined a requirement of 320 F-15s. In June, a contract was awarded for 175 production aircraft. They also decided to modify a P-61C into F-15 configuration, as the production photo planes were to be powered with the same turbosupercharged R-2800-C model engines as the P-61C was. This plane was like the XF-15 except for the powerplant, and its canopy slid back like the Number 2 XP-61E. P-61C-1, serial number 43-8335, was accepted by the AAF at Northrop Field on Aug. 10, 1945, and was taken almost immediately into the Northrop modification shop where it underwent almost the identical surgery as did the XP-61E/ XF-15. On Oct. 17, 1945, Northrop test pilot Max Stanley took it into the air for the first time.

An interesting statement in Northrop Specification 20A, which covers the F-15A-1 production aircraft, was that they would be essentially a modification of the P-61C, and that they would

employ the use of P-61C parts and assemblies. Feeling either that they lacked in expertise or were at capacity in engineering, or both, Northrop elected to subcontract the redesign of the camera nose to Hughes Tool Company of Culver City, California. Overseeing this project for Northrop was project engineer Willard R. "Pappy" Clay. As with the XF-15A, the F-15A-1 planes consisted of a major modification of the standard Black Widow crew nacelle, and the elim-

ination of the fighter brakes from the wings.

The first production aircraft was accepted in September 1946. For reasons unclear, possibly that the F-15 was overtaken by technology, the contract was cancelled abruptly in 1947. A total of thirty-six aircraft were accepted—the last being in April of that year. In March 1947 a supplement had been added to NS-20A which called for the last F-15 (serial number 45-59335) to

The second XP-61E's gun nose on a test stand for firing tests. Like its night fighter variants, it retained the four 20 mm cannons in its belly. Unfortunately, the second E was lost in an accident just about a month after this photo was taken. Balzer

The second XP-61E differed from the first in that it had a horizontal, rather than boxed, gun configuration. The hinged canopy of the first E was replaced by a canopy which slid back on tracks along the top of the fuselage. Balzer

This damage to XP-61E, serial number 42-39557, occurred in April 1945 when an Army Air Forces day fighter pilot assigned to the Northrop plant pulled his gear before attaining sufficient air speed for takeoff.

The unfortunate result was the plane settling down to the runway. The pilot walked away with minor injuries, and was soon reassigned. The plane was a complete write-off. Balzer

be produced as an F-15A-5. This change was an internal one in camera operation and installation. Apparently as early as mid-1946, this change had been contemplated for the last twenty F-15s. Some records indicate that these were all eventually redesignated as F-15A-5s.

Nine of the planes were initially assigned to Air Materiel Command. The remaining twenty-seven went to Japan and were operated by the 8th Photo Reconnaissance Squadron (PRS) flying out of Johnson Air Base. The first four were sent over by ship, arriving in March 1947 at the Japan Air Materiel Area (JAMA), Kisarazu, Japan. Their voyage had not been smooth, however. Three of the four were in such sad shape that they were turned into spare parts.

P-61, serial number 42-39549, after its modification to XP-61E, underwent further modifications to XF-15 as its guns were

replaced by aerial cameras. The yellow cowl and spinner shown on this beautiful in-flight shot of the XF-15 Reporter were stan-

dard for Northrop flight-test aircraft. Wolford

The 8th PRS, which had been non-operational for about a year, was being manned up to strength in preparation to become part of the Post-Hostilities Mapping Program. Along with other similar units, the 8th's part in the program was to take beach and cultural photographs (villages, road networks and similar type features). An associated part of the program was the long-range/high-altitude work of the F-13/B-29 type photo units.

Under the command of Maj. Benjamin H. Albertson, the 8th PRS spent most of the summer of 1947 preparing for the missions to come. During June and July, a crew was maintained at JAMA assisting in the assembling of the F-15s. Captain Jarvis and Lieutenant Heistand were the two lucky pilots to pick up the squadron's first pair of Reporters in late June. They spent most of July test flying their newly assembled planes. Four additional aircraft that month helped the pilots to accumulate a total of seventy-three hours. The unit's first mission was flown that same month, with Captain Moore at the controls.

The remainder of 1947 saw a noted increase in the tempo of activity. Unfortunately, the squadron lost its first F-15 in August when a pilot made a very hard landing. The plane was a write-off but the pilot walked away.

Lt. Col. Ben K. Armstrong became commanding officer in September. Unit strength of sixteen aircraft was reached in October. Also during October, a detachment of three aircraft and crews was sent to Itazuke AAB on Kyushu. Their mission was to fly four- to seven-hour missions. The detachment was maintained there into December 1947.

Activity remained at a high rate with the coming of the new year. A detachment of six aircraft was sent to Clark Field in the Philippines in January 1948 to assist the 5th Reconnaissance Group. As time went on, other detachments were sent out to Itazuke and Chitose Air Bases for varying lengths of time. The longest time out was for the detachment under Thirteenth Air Force in the Philippines, which continued until early September. Here the crews were rotated every thirty days.

Maintaining the aircraft became a problem early in the program. In January 1948 the F-15s were grounded for ten days because of weather and a lack

of parts. The main problem was with the heat exchangers cracking. Due to the total lack of spare parts, heat exchangers were being removed from F-15s in storage at JAMA. The total support

This F-15 Reporter flew with the 8th PRS, indicated by the eight ball on the tail.

problem had become so critical that the 8th PRS had an average daily in-commission rate of only two aircraft throughout February. Cannibalization of both damaged and flyable aircraft eventually

The Missing Link, *serial number 45–59302, was one of the F–15As assigned to the 8th PRS in Japan. Note the snow on the aircraft.*

107

brought up the rate, but the unit never reached the strength of sixteen aircraft again; they only reached a high of fifteen in December 1948.

RF-61C

A number of changes occurred during 1948. Maj. Russell E. Cheever took over as squadron commander in April, and the unit was redesignated the 8th Tactical Reconnaissance Squadron (Night Photo) in August. Under the new US Air Force aircraft designation system, the F-15 (*F* designating Photo under AAF system) became the RF-61 (*R* for reconnaissance and *F* for fighter). But for a few months there was confusion. The designation RF-61A was carried erroneously both in USAF and squadron records; the proper RF-61C (as these aircraft were modified F-61Cs) was applied shortly thereafter.

The end of the Reporter's Air Force career came on Apr. 1, 1949. It was foretold on March 25, when the 8th TRS was transferred to Yokota AB, less equipment and personnel. In effect, what happened was that the 8th TRS became the 82nd and vice versa. On April 1, the

82nd (in reality the old 8th personnel and aircraft) was deactivated and all RF-61C aircraft were assigned to the 35th Maintenance Squadron at Johnson Air Base for salvage or other disposition.

There were three P-61 variants that almost were: the F, G and H models.

Item 9 of Supplemental Agreement Number 8 to contract W33-038 ac-2407 (the XP-61D contract) called for P-61C, serial number 43-8338, to be modified into a night fighter AAF Model XP-61F in accordance with Northrop Specification NS-21 dated June 1, 1945. The supplemental agreement also stipulated that Northrop was to carry out a ten-hour flight-test program to determine the plane's general flight characteristics, and that the XP-61F was to be delivered to the AAF no later than Sept. 1, 1945.

The Individual Aircraft Record Card for P-61C, serial number 43-8338, shows that the aircraft was accepted and delivered on Aug. 10, 1945, with the annotation, "To be retained at factory for conversion to two-place night fighter." Whether any modification work was performed or not is of some doubt. On

Oct. 24, 1945, the XP-61F contract was terminated, and a crew was requested on November 15 to fly the aircraft to the AMC storage facility at Independence Army Air Field in Kansas. The availability was deleted on December 6, and the plane was salvaged at Hawthorne before the end of the year.

The P-61G was a non-Northrop modification project. Sixteen P-61B-20s were sent to the Douglas Aircraft Co. modification center at Tulsa, Oklahoma, directly from the Northrop factory. Aircraft serial number 43-8298 arrived at Tulsa on June 15, 1945, and served as the mock-up for the project. The other P-61B-20s (serial numbers 43-8275, 8278-80, 8290-94, 8298, 8300-01, and 8303-06) all followed in that same month.

From what little evidence is available, the Western Electric-built SCR-720 AI radar was replaced by General Electric APS-10 "weather" radar. The dorsal turret was removed, and additional radio equipment and air sampling instruments were added. Contrary to some "official" reports, the black paint scheme was maintained—at least on some of the aircraft. By October 1945 fourteen of the aircraft were assigned to the 4185th AAF Base Unit at Independence Army Air Field. This base was basically an AMC long-term storage facility. Of the other two aircraft, serial number 43-8298 went from Tulsa back to the Northrop plant, and number 43-8304 remained at Tulsa until it was scrapped in December 1945. Except for the latter, all of the surviving fifteen planes joined AMC (Air Materiel Command) or ADC (Air Defense Command) units in 1946. It is of interest that the USAF's Individual Aircraft Record Cards for these aircraft do not reflect the G model designation.

Very little is known of the P-61H "dome tank" proposal. There had been talk early in the Black Widow program of deleting the turret and using the space created in the crew nacelle by this action for additional fuel. Apparently the "dome tank" project of mid-1945 did this and went a little further. In this proposal an aerodynamic dome extended above the normally flat crew nacelle top. It would seem, however, that this project did not go past the wind-tunnel model stage.

The top view of the P-61H Dome Tank. This model didn't make it past the wind-tunnel model stage. Northrop

Chapter 11

Peacetime Widow

Victory in Europe was decreed on May 8, 1945. War was still waging on the other side of the globe, which meant that many, if not most, of the armed forces were to be sent to new lands to fight another enemy. On V-E Day, five of the six AAF night fighter squadrons in the European and Mediterranean theaters were equipped with P-61s; the 416th NFS was flying the Mosquito Mk. 30. Most of these squadrons were soon scheduled to be sent directly to the Pacific, or rotated back to the States and then on to the Far East.

But a new weapon, the atomic bomb, helped to bring the great war against the Imperial Japanese Empire to a sudden halt. The ending of hostilities in August 1945 negated the transfer of the AAF night fighter units from across the Atlantic. The 414th, 422nd and 425th became nonoperational and were transferred back to the United States on paper, as were most of the personnel in these units. The 414th's Widows were turned over to the 416th, who in turn had sent on their beloved Mosquitoes to Great Britain.

On August 7 the United States Air Forces in Europe was organized. Its night fighter force consisted of the 415th NFS based at Nordholz, Germany; the 417th NFS at Kessel/Rothwestern, Germany; and in Austria, the 416th was stationed at Horsching. Most of the war-weary P-61s were scrapped at their last operational bases, and operational aircraft in excess of unit needs were sent to the storage facility at Oberpafrafe, Germany.

As in Europe, reorganization of the AAF's night fighter arm in the Pacific meant many changes. Before the end of

1945, the 426th, 427th, 548th and 550th were deactivated. As part of the occupational forces, the 418th and 547th were transferred from Okinawa and Ie Shima to Atsugi, and the 421st also from Ie Shima to Itazuke. Remaining at their last wartime stations were the 6th NFS in Hawaii, the 419th at Puerto Princesa on Palawan in the Philippines, and the 549th on Iwo Jima.

The US Army Air Forces were reorganized into three major operational commands on Mar. 21, 1946: Strategic Air Command (SAC), Tactical Air Command (TAC) and Air Defense Command (ADC). All three commands would initially be assigned Black Widow squadrons. To SAC came the 57th and 58th reconnaissance squadrons (weather); TAC got the 415th NFS (originally intended for SAC); and ADC received the 414th (soon to be transferred to TAC) and the 425th night fighter squadrons. All three night fighter squadrons were nonoperational units that had to be manned and equipped.

The 57th and 58th reconnaissance squadrons (weather) arrived at Rapid City Army Air Field (now Ellsworth AFB), South Dakota, in July 1945. At about this same time they started receiving early-model P-61Bs. These squadrons were part of the Third Air Force, whose duties were to train reconnaissance crews. As part of the mass changes of force structure within the AAF in 1946, the 57th was deactivated in January of that year and the 58th followed suit in May. One might wonder if the P-61B-20/P-61G conversion program might have been tied into plans for these two squadrons, and cancelled when the squadrons were deactivated.

In 1946, the 414th and 415th NFSs were reactivated and manned and equipped at Shaw Field, South Carolina. By early 1947 they were up to strength and operational. The 414th was transferred to Rio Hato in the Panama Canal Zone and reassigned to the Caribbean Air Command in March 1947. The 415th went in the opposite direction to Adak, Alaska, that May where it was reassigned to the Alaskan Air Command.

Taking on more of the standard structure of Air Force units, the three remaining night fighter squadrons in the Pacific—the 6th, 418th and 421st— were all grouped under and assigned to the 347th Fighter Group in February 1947. At this time the squadrons were all renumbered. They became the 339th,

These P-61s had been flown by the 417th NFS. They are now only remains of the once feared night hunters. These "war weary" aircraft are being scrapped at Schweinfurt, Germany, August 1947. Linsey

4th and 68th fighter squadrons, respectively. In August 1948, their designation was changed to Fighter Squadron (All Weather) to more closely identify their mission. In that same period, two non-operational squadrons, the 419th NFS in the Philippines and the 449th NFS on Guam, were deactivated.

A few months later, the 52nd FG was activated in Germany and took under its wing the 416th and 417th night fighter squadrons. As with the Pacific night fighter units, these squadrons were also renumbered. They became the 2nd and 5th fighter squadrons, respectively.

Air Defense Command was originally to get the 425th and 414th night fighter squadrons, but the 414th was reassigned to TAC before that squadron was reactivated. On Sept. 1, 1946, the inactive 425th NFS was transferred, on paper, to McChord Field, Washington, and remanning of the unit was started. The fledgling ADC was soon a two-squadron command—the P-61-equipped 425th NFS on the West Coast and a P-47 squadron on the East Coast.

The 325th FG, along with its 318th FS, was activated at Mitchel Field, New York, on May 21, 1947, doubling ADC's Black Widow squadron strength. A month later, the European 52nd FG (with its 2nd and 5th fighter squadrons) was transferred to Mitchel Field without personnel and aircraft. Reorganized and reequipped with Widows, the 52nd was soon an operational ADC unit. With the 52nd once again operational, the 325th Fighter Group was transferred to Hamilton Field in California, along with its 317th and 318th squadrons. The 319th FS (formerly the 414th NFS) in Panama was assigned to the 325th FG.

The useful life of the Black Widow had been extended due to the Air Force's problems in fielding a jet-powered night/all-weather fighter. The planners at AAF headquarters saw the P-61 being replaced by the Curtiss-Wright P-87 shortly after World War II. But due to problems with the jet all-weather fighter as well as its interim replacement, the North American P-82, the Widow flew into a new decade.

Replacement of ADC's F-61s by F-82F Twin Mustangs began in early 1948. Alaska's 449th FS (formerly the 415th NFS) received a special winterized version called the F-82H. Last to give up their now aged Widows were the squadrons of the 347th FG (AW) in the Pacific. Here, the F-61s were replaced by

An F-15 Reporter of the 8th PRS in 1948.

the F-82G between mid-1949 and 1950. The last operational Black Widow left its operational squadron in Japan in May 1950, less than a month from the breakout of hostilities in Korea.

Ejection Seat Program

The need for an emergency egress system from pusher-type aircraft had long been a concern of the AAF; but with the coming of the jet age, the need for an ejection system from conventional aircraft operating at high speeds was mandatory. Air Materiel Command had been experimenting with a catapult-type ejection seat which would safely get a pilot over the tail assembly and propeller of an aircraft with pusher propeller configuration. By April 1945, the AAF's Ordnance Department was at work on a rocket-ejection seat unit.

An ejection seat for a German He 162 was obtained by the Ordnance Department shortly after the end of hostilities. The seat was installed in a Lockheed P-80 in August 1945. After some amount of experimentation, it was felt that the seat could not meet certain requirements. A new catapult system was then designed and installed in P-61B-5, serial number 42-39498, on Oct. 4, 1945. This aircraft was subsequently redesignated XP-61B; it reverted back to its original designation of P-61B on Feb. 23, 1947.

The ejection seat was installed into the XP-61B on Oct. 19, 1945, in the forward gunner's compartment. Initial ground testing of the aircraft had it in a nose-high attitude. A dummy was used in the ground test phase.

With the new T-4 seats, the entire project was moved to Muroc Army Air Field, California, for flight testing. The aircraft, now dubbed *Jack-in-the-Box*, had camera observation lines painted along the fuselage side. The P-61 was flown at 150, 200, 240, 270 and 300 mph at an altitude of about 12,200 ft. Like the ground tests, a dummy was used initially. Then on Apr. 17, 1946, Sgt. Lawrence Lambert was ejected from the aircraft. This ejection was from 7,800 ft. and at a speed of 302 mph. With the concept proved, the newer jet powered aircraft for which the ejection seats were intended were brought into the program.

Thunderstorm Project

Congress allocated over $250,000 to the US Weather Bureau in 1945 to con-

An in-flight close-up of an F-61B of the 68th FIS over Bofu, Japan, in 1949. C. S. Frazer

The P-61B-5, serial number 42-39498, Jack-In-The-Box was named for its involvement in the ejection seat project. This is Cpl. Harry J. Brickheimer making his first jump with the aid of the newly developed ejection seat. Brickheimer was shot from the speeding P-61 at an altitude of approximately 5,000 ft. He was the second person to be shot out of the P-61. His jump followed the earlier jump of Sgt. Lawrence Lambert. USAF

Just as the Widow flew without hesitation into the relatively new field of night fighting, it also ventured bravely into weather fronts most aircraft avoided if at all possible. Project Thunderstorm was a great success.

Although it was just a beginning in understanding storm fronts the Widow had been there first and served well. Note the name Thunderstorm *on the front gear door of this P-61, serial number 43–8356.*

duct investigations into thunderstorms and associated hazards to aircraft. Many civilian and military agencies were to partake in this project. The AAF Board at Orlando Army Air Base, Florida, was in general supervision of Phase I. These operations were to be carried out at Pinecastle Army Airfield.

Phase I took place during the summer of 1946. The convective-type thunderstorms were quite common to the Orlando area. The powerful microwave early warning (MEW) stations were used to detect and track the thunderstorms. The project's aircraft was also tracked by MEW stations during penetration. Numerous observation stations were located in the area and were used to record meteorological conditions prior to, during and after the flights.

This RF-61C, serial number 45–59318, was also used in Project Thunderstorm. Its orig- *inal designation had been F-15A-1-NO. Under the wing on the boom is written "ALL* *WEATHER FLYING CENTER." This aircraft is mostly bare metal.*

Participating aircraft included nine P-61Cs flown by Air Force pilots. The aircraft were modified to carry AAF, MIT, NACA and Navy measuring and recording instrumentation. A 16 mm motion picture recording camera was installed that would photograph the pilot's instrument panel.

The flights from Pinecastle took place between June 29 and Sept. 18, 1946. The P-61s operated in flights of five in this phase. Once an incoming storm was detected approaching the test area, the Widows were scrambled. Penetration of the storm was at 5,000 ft. intervals, starting around 5,000 ft. with the top flight, going to about 25,000 ft. One aircraft had the double task of photographing the thundercloud and flying numerous circles around it. The exact location and dimension of the cloud could be obtained by using the radar plot of this plane.

Phase II of Project Thunderstorm was the investigation of frontal-type thunderstorms carried out at Clinton County Army Air Field, Ohio. Overseeing this phase was the All Weather Flying Division. The project arrived at Clinton County AAFld. on Feb. 10, 1947. The

Quasimodo, *named for its hunched back, was assigned to NACA for weather testing in Alaska.* Northrop via Balzer

P-61C force was increased to thirteen, along with the addition of the XF-15, XF-15A and two production F-15As. The P-61Cs had their turbo regulators and exhaust stack bolts modified at Tinker Field, Oklahoma, before starting this phase.

Phase II operations commenced on May 1, 1947. A new participant was added when the project went to Ohio—Trans World Airlines. P-61B-25, serial number 43-8231, was bailed to TWA by the Air Force and was flown by TWA Capt. Robert N. Buck during the Ohio operations. The old adage concerning thunderstorms was: "Avoid them if possible. If you can't, then pray and pray hard." But the airlines had to have a lot more to go on than that, and that is the reason for TWA's involvement in Project Thunderstorm. Buck remembers, "It [the P-61] was a great airplane. I enjoyed flying it, even in the middle of a thunderstorm; and we flew quite a number of them." He accumulated about seventy-five flight hours that summer.

The project lasted throughout the summer of 1947. The F-15 aircraft were used in lightning strike tests, both within the thunderhead and manmade on the ground, and for high-altitude penetration of the storms. The last official flight occurred on September 15. The project was shut down in October. The All Weather Flying Division carried out still further flights the following summer.

A great quantity of data had been amassed by the time the project ended in late 1947. Preliminary analysis was made at the University of Chicago, and voluminous reports were produced by the agencies participating in the project.

Port, starboard and front views of the modified weather recon nose radar installation on the Weather Widow.

*This F-15A, serial number 45–59300, saw
duty with the National Advisory Committee
for Aeronautics (NACA).*

A new frontier had been penetrated; there would be much more to come.

NACA

In 1944, the National Advisory Committee for Aeronautics (NACA) started investigating the reliability of the drag data for airplanes at high Mach numbers which had been obtained in wind-tunnel tests. Flight-test data of an actual aircraft was needed to be compared to its wind-tunnel equivalent. NACA's Ames Aeronautical Laboratory at Moffett Field, California, was selected as the test site. A North American P-51B-1 Mustang was chosen along with a ⅓ scale wind-tunnel model.

The P-51 was highly instrumented. Its propeller and bomb racks were removed, and it was shellacked and waxed. P-61A-10 (serial number 42-5572) was chosen to tow the P-51 to altitude. The P-61 towed it to altitudes between 25,000 and 30,000 ft., where the P-51 was released and the pilot dove at near-supersonic speeds. Between September and October 1944, the Widow took the P-51 to release point on four occasions. Unfortunately, the fourth flight ended with the destruction of the Mustang. The data obtained from the instrumented P-51 confirmed that the wind-tunnel-based calculations predicted the Mustang's drag characteristic satisfactorily.

Many military aircraft were test flown by the NACA to obtain aerodynamic data and to determine handling qualities. P-61A-10, serial number 42-5572, arrived at NACA's Moffett Field on Apr. 27, 1944, for this purpose. It participated in the P-51 tow test already mentioned, and in later turret buffet tests.

On Feb. 6, 1948, NACA obtained an RF-61C (originally designated F-15), serial number 45-59300, from the US Air Force. Its mission was to take recoverable aerodynamic bodies to altitude, then drop them. Much was learned of swept-wing technology from these tests.

The same F-15A, with registration number N9768Z, was converted to a borate bomber. While it was owned by Cal-Nat Airways it wore both the yellow and white, and later it was painted orange and white for its fire-fighting missions. It shared the fate of its sister fire-fighting Widow when it crashed in September 1968 in California.

The colorful tail feathers of N9768Z. Killian

Another of the F-15As, 45-59300, would change its designation to RF-61C. This aircraft was used by NACA to take recoverable *aerodynamic bodies to altitude, then drop them to study swept-wing technology.*

This program continued into 1953. At the end of testing, the P-61 was returned to the USAF.

In late 1950 NACA felt that an additional plane was needed for use in their drop tests. Arrangements were made for the loan of an F-61C that had been donated to the Smithsonian Institution in October 1950 and which was still airworthy, and the aircraft was soon on its way to the West Coast. F-61C, serial number 43-8330, was on loan to NACA Ames from Feb. 15, 1951, to Aug. 9, 1954. It was then returned to the Smithsonian.

These two aircraft were fitted with special racks to carry various sweptwing bodies. Over the 4½ years of this project, the two aircraft dropped recoverable aerodynamic bodies from 40,000 ft. The actual drops were conducted over Edwards Air Force Base bomb drop range in the Mojave Desert, California.

Two other F-61s were used by NACA. F-61C, serial number 43-8357, was stationed at Ames between July 13, 1951, and April 1955. It was used mostly as a source of spare parts for other RF/F-61C aircraft. F-61B-15, serial number 42-39754, was at NACA's Lewis

Flight Propulsion Laboratory in Cleveland, Ohio. This aircraft test flew airfoil-type ramjets during the 1947-48 period.

Civilian and Display Widows

Five P-61/F-15 aircraft have held civilian registration. One, P-61B-1, serial number 42-39419, spent nearly its entire military life bailed to Northrop. Northrop vice president John Myers made arrangements with the government at the end of World War II to purchase the plane. Registration number NX30020 was assigned to this, the first civilian Widow. It was used as an executive transport, flight-test chase plane, and in experiments with advanced navigational equipment.

The Jack Ammann Photogrammetric Engineers, a photo-mapping company based in San Antonio, Texas, purchased the plane in the early 1950s from Northrop. It was used by that company until shortly after the death of Ammann in mid-1961. At that time a merger took place followed by financial problems, and the Widow soon laid derelict. Next it was consigned to Aircraft Sales, Ltd. of Los Angeles, California. They offered to convert it to a seven-passenger "executive" airplane, but there were no takers. Ranchers Incorporated purchased the airplane for use as an air tanker in February 1963. A 1,600 gallon chemical tank was installed, and on April 19 the Widow received its airworthiness certificate (restricted category).

On Aug. 23, 1963, a raging forest fire broke out on the Tule River Indian Reservation southeast of Porterville, California. Among the many aircraft called in by the California State Division of Forestry was the Widow. Flying the plane was veteran 421st NFS pilot Robert E. Savaria. Savaria dropped his first load of benetonite at 2:30 pm. By 4:30 pm, the fifth run of the day was being made. The right wing tip struck three oak trees about twelve feet above ground level. The plane cartwheeled and burst into flames, killing Savaria and destroying the last flying P-61.

A YP-61, serial number 41-18888, was purchased by Pratt & Whitney Aircraft from Military Surplus on June 6, 1946. Registration number N60358 was assigned by the Civil Aeronautics Authority. The plane was used as a flying testbed for aircraft engines, propellers and associated equipment. The Widow

was accidentally taxied into a whirling propeller in June 1956, severely damaging the cockpit area. Pratt & Whitney determined the Widow was not worth repairing and sent it to be scrapped.

Another YP-61, serial number 41-18878, almost made it to a museum. Scheduled to go to the Air Force Museum (AFM), it was stored at Davis-Monthan Field, Arizona, awaiting disposition in the late 1940s. Apparently AFM opted for a P-61C, so it was offered to the Smithsonian Institution in early 1950. Expenses required to refurbish the aircraft led the Smithsonian to reject the YP-61. P-61C, serial number 43-8330, was accepted by the Smithsonian in lieu of the YP-61. In about November 1950, Davis-Monthan scrapped the old bird.

Northrop Aeronautical Institute (NAI), a part of Northrop Aircraft Co., purchased a P-61C, serial number 43-8349, in late 1947. At NAI the plane, known as *Old Smokey*, was used in the airframe and engine maintenance pro-

This red and white Widow XB-FUJ was used for mapping. Baker

previous page
Formally P-61B-1, serial number 42–39419, the registration number assigned to this Widow purchased by Northrop vice president John Myers was N30020. It was used for photo-mapping while wearing this paint scheme.

gram. In 1963 the school was sold by Northrop and many planes were turned over to the General Services Administration. Bob Bean Aircraft, also located on Northrop Field, purchased the P-61C. They thought they could make it airworthy again. Civilian registration number N4905V was obtained even before they gave it a hard look. Upon inspecting the plane, however, they found it so full of corrosion that they deemed it not worth fixing. The engines were removed and sold. In about 1955 they scrapped the airframe.

NACA's Ames Laboratory felt that their F-15A, serial number 45-59300, was in excess of their needs and required more maintenance than it was worth. It and their "spare parts" P-61C, number 43-8357, were scheduled for the scrap yard in early 1955. In April 1955, Steward-Davis Inc. of Gardena, California, purchased both of the planes and towed them to nearby San Jose Airport. The F-15 was made flyable and was flown to southern California, where it underwent a complete overhaul. The P-61C, licensed N5094V, didn't fare as well. Steward-Davis offered it for sale, completely rebuilt, as a high-altitude

P-61 N30020 changed from bronze to this yellow and black paint scheme, and an underslung belly tank was added for its new assignment as a fire bomber. It crashed in California in August 1963. Michael O'Leary

aerial mapping plane. By 1957 no one wanted it, so it was junked.

With its civilian registration of N5093V, the F-15 was issued an airworthiness certificate as an aerial survey aircraft on July 16, 1956. That September, Luis Struck of Compania Mexicana Aerofoto, S.A., Mexico City, Mexico, purchased the plane and had it flown to Mexico shortly afterward. In Mexico it was registered XB-FUJ. After being purchased by Aero Enterprises, Inc. of Willets, California, serial number 45-59300

reentered the United States in January 1964. It now carried US registration number N9768Z. The fuselage fuel tank and turbosupercharger intercoolers were removed, and it was flown to the Cal-Nat Airways' shop at Grass Valley, California. There, a 1,600 gallon chemical tank was added for fire-fighting. By year's end, Cal-Nat had purchased the plane.

For the next 3½ years Cal-Nat operated the F-15 out of Fresno, California. Three different types of Hamilton

Standard Hydromatic propellers were installed in place of the plane's original Curtiss Electric propellers in an attempt at improving the aircraft's takeoff performance.

TBM, Inc. of Tulare, California, purchased the F-15 in March 1968. Pilot Ralph M. Ponte took off from Fresno Airport with a load of Phoscheck fire retardant to drop in the foothills near Hollister, California, on Sept. 6, 1968. Ponte was ready to leave Hollister with a third load of fire retardant that evening.

It was still very hot and the air was extremely light. The F-15A had a full load. He apparently obtained full power but never left the ground. He went full bore through a vegetable patch, wiping off the landing gear on a bank. He slid sideways, broke up and caught fire.

A B-17 pilot on the ground, watching this in great amazement, broadcast blind on the forestry frequency to any airborne tanker with a full load to give assistance. A TBM Avenger that was airborne at the time received the emergency message and turned back to the field. The pilot, Carl Kennedy, lowered the Avenger's nose and roared down toward the towering black smoke. He dropped half a load on one engine, turned around and dumped the other half on the other engine and boom area. If it hadn't been for Kennedy's quick response, the F-15 pilot probably would have been killed.

There are presently three P-61s on display. The Smithsonian's National Air and Space Museum has their P-61C at their storage facility at Silver Hill, Maryland, awaiting some much-needed restoration. The Air Force Museum's P-61C has been stationed at Wright Field, Ohio, for most of its service life. On May 9, 1949, it was donated to the Tecumseh Council of the Boy Scouts of America in Springfield, Ohio. The scouts placed it on display in a grassy field outside of Grimes Airport in Urbana, Ohio. On June 20, 1957, the scouts donated the Widow to the Air Force Museum at Wright-Patterson AFB, Ohio. The museum has accomplished a good bit of restoration work on this aircraft.

The third Widow, a P-61A, is on display at the Beijing Institute of Aeronautical Engineering in Beijing, China. A professor at that institute has explained: "Several P-61s of the US Air Force were stationed at air bases in Szechwan Province during the war. When the war ended, one of these P-61s was turned over to the Chendu Institute of Aeronautical Engineering in 1947. When the Institute moved to its new location, they did not take the plane with them. Instead, it was shipped to the Air Museum at the Beijing Institute of Aeronautical Engineering in 1954."

It has been reported by some of the former members of the 427th Night Fighter Squadron, one of two night fighter squadrons to serve in China during World War II, that there is a little more to the story. It seems that at the end of hostilities, the squadron was in the process of bringing their various detachments back to a central airfield for disposition of the aircraft and to start processing home. At one of the satellite fields there were a number of squadron members plus three P-61s, two in need of maintenance. Reportedly, some Chinese communist troops came onto the field and ordered the Americans to leave—but leave their aircraft behind. There are at least two groups here in the States that are trying to negotiate to bring back the Beijing Black Widow. In their negotiations with Chinese officials, there has also been the hint that this was one of the three confiscated, and that there might be others (or remains of others).

The remains of three P-61s in New Guinea have been known of for quite a few years. Two of them are in the Vogelkop area. One is a P-61A-1, serial number 42-5515. It belonged to the 419th NFS and was reported missing in action on Oct. 18, 1944. The other is reportedly a P-61A-5, serial number 42-5562. The unit of origin is unknown at this time. The third aircraft is a P-61B-1, serial number 42-39445. It belonged to the 550th NFS and crashed on Jan. 10, 1945. This craft is presently being recovered from its resting place of many years on Mt. Cyclopes, by the Mid Atlantic Air Museum of Middletown, Pennsylvania.

This P-61 is the only known Black Widow in China. It is now on display at a small aircraft museum and vocational technical school. K.C. Wu

Appendix A

Black Widow Squadrons

6th NFS

Activated: Redesignated 6th NFS on Jan. 18, 1943 (was the 6th FS)

Inactivated: Feb. 20, 1947 (became 339th FS)

Stations: Kipapa Gulch, TH Nov. 17, 1942-Mar. 3, 1944
Det. Guadalcanal, Feb. 28-Dec. 15, 1943
Det. New Guinea, Apr. 18-Dec. 15, 1943
John Rogers Field, TH Mar. 3-Oct. 28, 1944
Det. Saipan, June 21, 1944-May 1, 1945
Det. Iwo Jima
Kipapa Gulch, TH Oct. 28, 1944-Oct. 2, 1945
Wheeler Field, TH Oct. 2, 1945

Commanding officers:

Lt. James R. Watt (later Maj.)	Sept. 27, 1941-Sept. 14, 1942
Capt. Sidney F. Wharton	Sept. 14, 1942-Feb. 18, 1943
Capt. Victor M. Mahr	Feb. 18-Apr. 11, 1943
Capt. Julius E. Alford (acting)	Apr. 12-May 1, 1943
Capt. Victor M. Mahr	May 1-June 15, 1943
Capt. Julius E. Alford (acting)	June 16-July 7, 1943
Maj. Victor M. Mahr	July 8, 1943-Apr. 1, 1944
Maj. Julius E. Alford	Apr. 1-Apr. 15, 1944
Maj. Victor M. Mahr[3]	Apr. 15-May 15, 1944
Maj. Julius E. Alford	May 15, 1944-date unknown
Capt. Mark E. Martin	Date unknown-Dec. 18, 1944
1st Lt. Robert T. Merrill III	Dec. 18, 1944-Jan. 11, 1945
Capt. Mark E. Martin	Jan. 11-Mar. 7, 1945
Capt. George W. Mulholland	Mar. 7, 1945-Oct. 1945

- First P-61 received: May 1, 1944
- First enemy aircraft destroyed by P-61 crew: June 20, 1944
- Squadron total enemy aircraft destroyed by P-61 crews: 16

414th NFS

Activated: Jan. 26, 1943

Inactivated: Aug. 31, 1947 (became 319th FS)

Stations: La Senia, Algeria, May 10-June 11, 1943
Rerhaia, Algeria, June 11-Nov. 11, 1943
Note: The air echelon arrived at Rerhaia from their stay at RAF OTU in England in late July.
Det. Protville, Tunisia, July 23-29, 1943
Elmas, Sardinia, Nov. 11, 1943-June 22, 1944
Det. Ghisonaccia, Corsica, Jan. 9-Feb. 4, 1944; Mar. 20-July 15, 1944
Det. Borgo, Corsica, Feb. 5-July 15, 1944
Det. Alghero, Sardinia, May 11-June 22, 1944
Alghero, Sardinia, June 22-Sept. 5, 1944
Borgo, Corsica, Sept. 5-Oct. 13, 1944
Pisa, Italy, Oct.13-Nov. 25, 1944

Pontedera, Italy, Nov. 25, 1944-July 15, 1945
Det. Florennes, Belgium, Jan. 27-Apr. 3, 1945
Strossfeld, Germany, Apr. 3-23, 1945
Note: The above detachment operated in conjunction with the 422nd NFS of the Ninth AF.

Commanding officers:

Maj. Arden W. Cowgill	Jan. 26-Sept. 16, 1943
Maj. Earl T. Smith	Sept. 16, 1943-June 1, 1944
Lt. Col. Carroll H. Bolender	June 1, 1944-Jan. 21, 1946

- First P-61 received: Dec. 20, 1944
- First enemy aircraft destroyed by P-61 crew: Feb. 4, 1945
- Squadron total enemy aircraft destroyed by P-61 crews: 5

415th NFS

Activated: Feb. 10, 1943

Inactivated: Sept. 1, 1947 (became 449th FS)

Stations: La Senia, Algeria, May 12-June 22, 1943
La Sebala, Tunisia, June 22-25, 1943
Monastir, Tunisia, June 25-July 29, 1943
Note: The air echelon arrived at Monastir from their stay at RAF OTU in England on July 3.
Det. Protville, Tunisia, July 23-29, 1943
La Sebala, Tunisia, July 29-Sept. 3, 1943
Cassibile, Sicily, Sept. 3-Nov. 5, 1943
Cantania, Sicily, Nov. 5-Dec. 26, 1943
Det. Montecorvino, Italy, Nov. 29-Dec. 26, 1943
Det. Gaudo, Italy, Dec. 6, 1943-Jan. 30, 1944
Montecorvino, Italy, Dec. 26, 1943-Jan. 30, 1944
Marcianise, Italy, Jan. 30-Mar. 25, 1944
Pomigliano, Italy, Mar. 25-June 11, 1944
La Blanca, Italy, June 11-17, 1944
Valtone, Italy, June 17-July 9, 1944
Solonzara, Corsica, July 9-Sept. 1, 1944
Det. Piombino, Italy, July 23-Aug. 5, 1944
La Vallon, France, Sept. 1-25, 1944
Longvic, France, Sept. 25-Nov. 30, 1944
Ochey, France, Dec. 30, 1944-Mar. 18, 1945
St. Dizier, France, Mar. 18-Apr. 17, 1945
Gross-Gerau, Germany, Apr. 17, 1945-Oct. 2, 1945

Commanding Officers:

Capt. Gordon D. Timmons	Feb. 10, 1943-Aug. 31, 1944
Maj. Harold F. Augspurger	Aug. 31, 1944-Feb. 15, 1946

- First P-61 received: Mar. 20, 1945
- First enemy aircraft destroyed by P-61 crew: none
- Squadron total enemy aircraft destroyed by P-61 crews: 0

418th NFS

Activated: Apr. 1, 1943
Inactivated: Feb. 20, 1947 (became 4th FS)
Stations: Milne Bay, New Guinea, Nov. 2-22, 1943
Dobodura, New Guinea, Nov. 22, 1943-Mar. 28, 1944
Finschhafen, New Guinea, Mar. 28-May 12, 1944
Hollandia, New Guinea, May 12-Sept. 28, 1944
Det. Wakde Island, June 8-Aug. 18, 1944 (start of B-25 operations)
Det. Owi Island, Sept. 16-Oct. 5, 1944
Morotai, Halmaheras, NEI, Sept. 28-Dec. 26, 1944
Det. Dulag, Leyte, PI, Nov. 14-30, 1944
San Jose, Mindoro, PI, Dec. 15-26, 1944
Note: The above detachments were the squadron's ground echelon only.
San Jose, Mindoro, PI, Dec. 26, 1944-July 26, 1945
Det. Sanga Sanga Island, Sulu Arch., June-July 1945
Okinawa, July 26-Oct. 6, 1945

Commanding officers:

Maj. Carroll C. Smith	Apr. 1, 1943-Feb. 15, 1945
Capt. William B. Sellers	Feb. 15-Nov. 1945

- First P-61 received: early September 1944
- First enemy aircraft destroyed by P-61 crew: Oct. 7, 1944
- Squadron total enemy aircraft destroyed by P-61 crews: 18

419th NFS

Activated: Apr. 1, 1943
Inactivated: Feb. 20, 1947
Stations: Guadalcanal, Solomons, Nov. 15, 1943-July 17, 1944
Det. A. Bougainville, Solomons, Jan. 25-Mar. 27, 1944
Det. A Nadzab, New Guinea, June 27-July 25, 1944
Det. B Momote, Los Negros, Admiraltys, June 28-Aug. 18, 1944
Det. A Noemfoor Island, NEI, July 25-Nov. 27, 1944
HQ Det. Middelburg Island, NEI, Aug. 18, 1944-Feb. 10, 1945
Det. A Morotai, Halmaheras, NEI, Nov. 27, 1944-Mar. 16, 1945
HQ Det. Puerto Princesa, Palawan, PI, Mar. 6-Aug. 31, 1945
Det. A. Zamboanga, Mindanao, PI, Mar. 16-July 20, 1945
Det. B. Sanga Sanga, Sulu Arch., June 20-July 27, 1945
Puerto Princesa, Palawan, PI, July 27, 1945-Jan. 10, 1946

Commanding Officers:

Capt. John J. McCloskey	Apr. 1-Nov. 22, 1943
Maj. Ralph F. Jones	Nov. 23-Dec. 22, 1943
Capt. Emerson Y. Barker	Dec. 22, 1943-Jan. 16, 1944
Maj. Ralph F. Jones	Jan. 17-Apr. 8, 1944
Capt. Emerson Y. Barker	Feb. 20-Apr. 8, 1944
Capt. Howard G. Daniel	Apr. 8-12, 1944
Maj. Emerson Y. Barker	Apr. 12-June 12, 1944
Capt. Al Lukas	June 13-15, 1944
Maj. Andrew J. Bing	June 16-30, 1944
Maj. Joseph A. Shulmistras	July 1, 1944-Jan. 30, 1945
Capt. Richard O. Stewart	Feb. 1-April 1945
Lt. Col. Norman M. Jacob	April-Nov. 1945

- First P-61 received: May 3, 1944

- First enemy aircraft destroyed by P-61 crew: Aug. 5, 1944
- Squadron total enemy aircraft destroyed by P-61 crews: 5

421st NFS

Activated: May 1, 1943
Inactivated: Feb. 20, 1947 (became 68th FS)
Stations: Milne Bay, New Guinea, Jan. 4-27, 1944
Nadzab, New Guinea, Jan. 27-June 28, 1944
Det. Wakde Island, May 28-Sept. 21, 1944
Owi Island, Schouten Islands, June 28-Oct. 25, 1944
Tacloban, Leyte, PI, Oct. 25, 1944-Feb. 8, 1945
Det. (air echelon) Peleliu, Palau Group, Dec. 3, 1944-Jan. 11, 1945
San Marcelino, Luzon, PI, Feb. 3-Apr. 26, 1945 (ground echelon arrived Feb. 3, followed by most of the air echelon Feb. 8)
Det. Tacloban, Leyte, PI, Feb. 9-Mar. 23, 1945
Clark Field, Luzon, PI, Apr. 26-Aug. 5, 1945
Ie Shima, Ryukyus, Aug. 8-Nov. 25, 1945

Commanding officers:

Maj. Walter S. Pharr	May 1, 1943-May 15, 1944
Capt. William T. Bradley	May 15, 1944-Jan. 2, 1945
Capt. Paul R. Zimmer	Jan. 2-15, 1945
Lt. Dorrie E. Jones	Jan. 15-20, 1945
Capt. Richard D. Kiick	Jan. 20-Dec. 15, 1945

- First P-61 received: June 1, 1944
- First enemy aircraft destroyed by P-61 crew: July 7, 1944
- Squadron total enemy aircraft destroyed by P-61 crews: 13

422nd NFS

Activated: Aug. 1, 1943
Inactivated: Sept. 30, 1945
Stations: Charmy Down, England, Mar. 7-May 6, 1944
Scorton, England, May 6-July 25, 1944
Det. Hurn Airdrome, England, June 28-July 11, 1944
Det. Ford Airdrome, England, July 16-26, 1944
Maupertu, France, July 25-Aug. 28, 1944
Chateaudun, France, Aug. 28-Sept. 16, 1944
Florennes, Belgium, Sept. 16, 1944-Apr. 6, 1945
Strassfeldt, Germany, Apr. 6-24, 1945
Langensalza, Germany, Apr. 24-May 26, 1945

Commanding officer:

Lt. Col. Oris B. Johnson	Aug. 1, 1943-Sept. 30, 1945

- First P-61 received: May 23, 1944
- First enemy aircraft destroyed by P-61 crew: July 16, 1944 (V-1); Aug. 7, 1944 (manned enemy aircraft)
- Squadron total enemy aircraft destroyed by P-61 crews: 43 manned; 5 V-1s

425th NFS

Activated: Dec. 1, 1943
Inactivated: Aug. 25, 1947 (became 317th FS)
Stations: Charmy Down, England, May 26-June 12, 1944
Scorton, England, June 12-Aug. 12, 1944
Det. Hurn Airdrome, England, June 29-July 1944
Stoneman Park, England, Aug. 12-18, 1944
Vanne, France, Aug. 18-Sept. 1, 1944
Le Moustier, France, Sept. 1-11, 1944
Coulommiers, France, Sept. 11-Oct. 13, 1944
Prosnes, France, Oct. 13-Nov. 19, 1944
Etain, France, Nov. 9, 1944-Apr. 12, 1945

Frankfurt, Germany, Apr. 12-May 2, 1945
Furth, Germany, May 2-July 5, 1945

Commanding officers:
Capt. Leon G. Lewis	Dec. 10, 1943-Feb. 10, 1945
Capt. Russell Glasser	Feb. 10-May 7, 1945
Capt. Morris T. McDonald	May 7, 1945-date unknown
Lt. Col. Leon G. Lewis	May-Sept. 1945

- First P-61 received: June 15, 1944
- First enemy aircraft destroyed by P-61 crew: Aug. 5, 1944 (V-1); Dec. 24, 1944 (manned enemy aircraft)
- Squadron total enemy aircraft destroyed by P-61 crews: 10 manned; 4 V-1s.

426th NFS

Activated:	Jan. 1, 1944
Inactivated:	Nov. 5, 1945
Stations:	Madhaiganj, India, Aug. 9-Oct. 5, 1944
	Chengtu, China, Oct. 5, 1944-Mar. 15, 1945
	Det. Kunming, China, Oct. 27-Dec. 25, 1944
	Det. Hsian, China, Nov. 27, 1944-Aug. 17, 1945
	Det. Guskhara, India, Jan.-Aug. 1945
	Shwangliu, China, Mar.-Sept. 1945
	Det. Liangshan, China, Apr.-Aug. 19, 1945
	Det. Ankang, China, Apr.-Aug. 21, 1945

Commanding Officer:
Maj. William C. Hellriegel	Jan. 1, 1944-Nov. 5, 1945

- First P-61 received: Sept. 25, 1944
- First enemy aircraft destroyed by P-61 crew: Oct. 29, 1944
- Squadron total enemy aircraft destroyed by P-61 crews: 5

427th NFS

Activated:	Feb. 1, 1944
Inactivated:	Oct. 29, 1945
Stations:	Pomigliano, Italy, Sept. 3-22, 1944
	Barrackpore, India (air echelon), Oct. 4-31, 1944
	Pandaveswar, India, Oct. 31-Dec. 23, 1944
	Det. Myitkyina, Burma, Nov. 13-Dec. 23, 1944
	Det. Kunming, China, Dec. 18, 1944-Aug. 16, 1945

Note: Elements of the Kunming detachment operated out of Chengkung, Chihkiang and Nanning at various periods during Jan.-Aug. 1945

	Myitkyina, Burma, Dec. 23, 1944-May 25, 1945
	Kisselbarri (near Dinjan), India, May 25-Aug. 13, 1945
	Liuchow, China, Aug. 13-Oct. 1945

Commanding officers:
Lt. Col. James S. Michael	Feb. 1, 1944-May 20, 1945
Maj. Thomas N. Wilson	May 21-June 1945
Maj. Edwin J. Witzenburger	June 1945-Oct. 29, 1945

- First P-61 received: mid-August 1944
- First enemy aircraft destroyed by P-61 crew: none
- Squadron total enemy aircraft destroyed by P-61 crews: 0

547th NFS

Activated:	Mar. 1, 1944
Inactivated:	Feb. 20, 1946
Stations:	Oro Bay, New Guinea, Sept. 5-Oct. 6, 1944
	Owi Island, Schouten Group, Oct. 6-Dec. 31, 1944
	Det. Tacloban, Leyte, PI, Nov. 9, 1944-Jan. 11, 1945
	Det. Mindoro, PI, Dec. 1944-Jan. 16, 1945
	Lingayen, Luzon, PI, Jan. 16-Aug. 13, 1945
	Ie Shima, Ryukyus, Aug. 13-Oct. 7, 1945

Commanding Officers:
Lt. Col. William C. Odell	Mar. 1, 1944-July 21, 1945
Capt. William C. Behnke	July 21-Nov. 11, 1945

- First P-61 received: Oct. 7, 1944
- First enemy aircraft destroyed by P-61 crew: Dec. 25, 1944
- Squadron total enemy aircraft destroyed by P-61 crews: 6

548th NFS

Activated:	Apr. 10, 1944
Inactivated:	Dec. 19, 1945
Stations:	Hickam Field, TH, Sept. 16-Oct. 17, 1944
	Kipapa Gulch, TH, Oct. 17, 1944-Jan. 26, 1945
	Det. Saipan, Dec. 15, 1944-Jan. 26, 1945
	Saipan, Jan. 26-Mar. 5, 1945
	Det. (ground echelon) Iwo Jima, Feb. 28-Mar. 5, 1945
	Iwo Jima, Mar. 5-June 12, 1945
	Ie Shima, June 12-Dec. 1, 1945

Commanding officer:
Maj. Robert D. Curtis	Apr. 10, 1944-Dec. 19, 1945

- First P-61 received: September 1944
- First enemy aircraft destroyed by P-61 crew: June 22, 1945
- Squadron total enemy aircraft destroyed by P-61 crews: 5

549th NFS

Activated:	May 1, 1944
Inactivated:	Feb. 5, 1946
Stations:	Kipapa Gulch, TH, Oct. 20, 1944-Feb. 15, 1945
	Saipan, Feb. 20-Mar. 20, 1945
	Det. (ground echelon) Iwo Jima, Mar. 14-20, 1945
	Iwo Jima, Mar. 20, 1945-Feb. 5, 1946

Commanding officers:
Maj. Joseph E. Payne	May 1, 1944-Sept. 25, 1945
Capt. William R. Charlesworth	Sept. 25, 1945-Jan. 16, 1946

- First P-61 received: October 1944
- First enemy aircraft destroyed by P-61 crew: June 23, 1945
- Squadron total enemy aircraft destroyed by P-61 crews: 1

550th NFS

Activated:	June, 1, 1944
Inactivated:	Jan. 4, 1946
Stations:	Hollandia, New Guinea, Dec. 14, 1944-Feb. 14, 1945
	Det. Middelburg Island, NEI, Dec. 31, 1944-Feb. 19, 1945
	Morotai, Halmaheras, NEI, Feb. 14-Apr. 7, 1945
	Det. Tacloban, Leyte, PI, Mar. 1-Apr. 7, 1945
	Tacloban, Leyte, PI, Apr. 7-Dec. 4, 1945
	Det. Zamboanga, Mindanao, PI, Apr. 27-June 17, 1945
	Det. Sanga Sanga, Sulu Arch., June 1-Aug. 1945
	Det. Puerto Princesa, Palawan, PI, June 9-19, 1945

Commanding officer:
Maj. Robert A. Tyler	June 1, 1944-Jan. 4, 1946

- First P-61 received: Jan. 6, 1945
- First enemy aircraft destroyed by P-61 crew: none
- Squadron total enemy aircraft destroyed by P-61 crews: 0

Appendix B

Aircrew Victories

The following information was derived from these sources (starting with the primary):
Headquarters USAF, Office of Air Force History
Champlin Fighter Museum
Orders of awards
Combat reports
Squadron histories

P-61 Aerial Victories

Air Force	Squadron	Confirmed kills	Air Force total
Fifth	418th NFS	18	
	421st NFS	13	
	547th NFS	6	
			37
Seventh	6th NFS	16	
	548th NFS	5	
	549th NFS	1	
			22
Ninth	422nd NFS	43[1]	
	425th NFS	10[2]	
			53[3]
Twelfth	414th NFS	5	
			5
Thirteenth	419th NFS	5	
			5
Fourteenth	426th NFS	5	
			5

[1]Plus 5 V-1s.
[2]Plus 4 V-1s.
[3]Plus 9 V-1s.

Confirmed Aircrew Victories

Aircrew	Squadron	Total kills	Notes
1st Lt. Herman E. Ernst (P)	422nd NFS	5	1 V-1 also
2nd Lt. Edward H. Kopsel (R/O)			
1st Lt. Robert A. Smith (P)	422nd NFS	5	1 V-1 also
1st Lt. Robert E. Tierney (R/O)			
Maj. Carroll C. Smith (P)	418th NFS	5	Smith has 2 in P-38s
1st Lt. Philip B. Porter (R/O)			
1st Lt. Eugene D. Axtell (P)	422nd NFS	5	
2nd Lt. Bernard Orzel (R/O)			2 E/A
2nd Lt. John U. Morris, Jr. (R/O)			1 E/A (3 total)
1st Lt. Creel H. Morrison (R/O)			2 E/A (4 total)
1st Lt. Robert G. Bolinder (P)	422nd NFS	4	
2nd Lt. Robert F. Graham (R/O)			(5 total)
Capt. Robert O. Elmore (P)	422nd NFS	4	1 V-1 also
2nd Lt. Leonard F. Mapes (R/O)			
1st Lt. Dale F. Haberman (P)	6th NFS	4	
2nd Lt. Raymond P. Mooney (R/O)			
Pvt. Patrick J. Farelly (G)			2 E/A
Capt. Owen M. Wolf (P)	421st NFS	4	
1st Lt. Byron N. Allain (R/O)			
T/Sgt. Emil K. Weishar (G)			3 E/A
S/Sgt. Donald H. Trabing (G)			1 E/A
Capt. Raymond A. Anderson (P)	422nd NFS	3	
2nd Lt. John U. Morris, Jr. (R/O)			2 E/A (3 total)
2nd Lt. Robert F. Graham (R/O)			1E/A (5 total)
1st Lt. Lewis A. Gordon (P)	422nd NFS	3	
F/O Joseph F. Crew (R/O)			2 E/A
2nd Lt. Creel H. Morrison (R/O)			1 E/A (4 total)
2nd Lt. Cletus T. Ormsby (P)	422nd NFS	3	3 more possibles

Confirmed Aircrew Victories

Aircrew	Squadron	Total kills	Notes
2nd Lt. Davis M. Howerton, Jr. (R/O)			
1st Lt. Albert R. Sorbo (P)	418th NFS	3	
2nd Lt. George N. Kerstetter (R/O)			
2nd Lt. Bertram C. Tompkins (P)	418th NFS	3	
F/O Vincent Wertin (R/O)			
1st Lt. John W. Anderson (P)	422nd NFS	2	1 V–1 also
2nd Lt. James W. Mogan (R/O)			
Capt. Tadas J. Spelis (P)	422nd NFS	2	1 V–1 also
1st Lt. Eleutherios Eleftherion (R/O)			
Capt. Carl J. Absmeier (P)	426th NFS	2	
2nd Lt. James R. Smith (R/O)			
1st Lt. William A. Andrews (P)	425th NFS	2	
2nd Lt. James E. Kleinheinz (R/O)			
2nd Lt. Carl H. Bjorum (P)	421st NFS	2	
2nd Lt. Robert C. Williams (R/O)			
S/Sgt. Henry E. Bobo (G)			
1st Lt. Arthur D. Bourque (P)	547th NFS	2	
2nd Lt. Bonnie B. Rucks (R/O)			(3 total)
1st Lt. Francis C. Eaton (P)	6th NFS	2	
2nd Lt. James E. Ketchum (R/O)			
S/Sgt William S. Anderson III (G)			1 E/A
2nd Lt. Donald T. Evans (P)	6th NFS	2	
2nd Lt. Nicholas R. DeVita (R/O)			
Cpl. Raymond L. Golden (G)			
Lt. Col. Oris B. Johnson (P)	422nd NFS	2	
Capt. James A. Montgomery (R/O)			
Capt. Albert L. Jones (P)	414th NFS	2	1 E/A in Beaufighter
2nd Lt. John E. Rudovsky (R/O)			
1st Lt. Theodore I. Jones (P)	422nd NFS	2	
1st Lt. William G. Adams, Jr. (R/O)			
Capt. Leonard F. Koehler (P)	422nd NFS	2	
1st Lt. Louis L. Bost (R/O)			
1st Lt. Albert W. Lockard (P)	421st NFS	2	
2nd Lt. Stuart A. Thornton (R/O)			
S/Sgt. Joseph Mazur (G)			
2nd Lt. Myrle W. McCumber (P)	6th NFS	2	
F/O Daniel L. Hinz (R/O)			
Pvt. Peter Dutkanicz (G)			1 E/A
S/Sgt. Benjamin J. Boscardin (G)	548th NFS		1 E/A (2 tot.
2nd Lt. James R. McQueen, Jr. (P)	418th NFS	2	
2nd Lt. Hugh L. Gordon (R/O)			
1st Lt. Jack E. Slayton (P)	425th NFS	2	
2nd Lt. Arthur B. Ferris (R/O)			1 E/A
1st Lt. Jack W. Robinson (R/O)			1 E/A (2 tot.
Capt. Ernest R. Thomas (P)	6th NFS	2	
1st Lt. John P. Acre (R/O)			
Cpl. Jesse V. Tew (G)	548th NFS		1 E/A (2 tot.
Capt. Francis V. Sartanowicz (P)	425th NFS	1	1 V–1 also
1st Lt. Edward M. Van Sickels (R/O)			
Capt. Edwin C. Annis (P)*	547th NFS	1	
2nd Lt. Nicholas Detz (R/O)			
1st Lt. Robert O. Bertram (P)	548th NFS	1	
2nd Lt. George W. Fairweather (R/O)			
Cpl. Jesse V. Tew (G)			(2 total)
Capt. Robert C. Blackman (P)	547th NFS	1	
1st Lt. Jean B. Harper (R/O)			
Capt. James W. Bradford (P)	548th NFS	1	
1st Lt. Lawrence K. Lunt, Jr. (R/O)			
M/Sgt. Reno H. Sukow (G)			
1st Lt. Thomas H. Burleson (P)	422nd NFS	1	

Confirmed Aircrew Victories

Aircrew	Squadron	Total kills	Notes	Aircrew	Squadron	Total kills	Notes
2nd Lt. William P. Monahan (R/O)				1st Lt. Dorrie E. Jones (P)	421st NFS	1	
1st Lt. Fred E. Burnett (P)	422nd NFS	1		1st Lt. Alton C. Woodring (R/O)			
F/O Clifford E. Brandt (R/O)				S/Sgt. Lacy Potter (G)			
1st Lt. James C. Crumley (P)	6th NFS	1		1st Lt. Ralph R. LeVitt (P)	419th NFS	1	
Lt. Jean B. Desclos (R/O)				2nd Lt. Frederic J. Kahn (R/O)			
Pvt. Otis H. O'Hair (G)				S/Sgt. John O. Graham (G)			
Capt. William H. Dames (P)	548th NFS	1		Capt. Alphonse Lukas (P)	419th NFS	1	
2nd Lt. Eugene P. D'Andrea (R/O)				2nd Lt. John S. Blankenship, Jr. (R/O)			
Sgt. Raymond C. Ryder (G)				S/Sgt. Glen O. DeForrest (G)			
1st Lt. Donald M. Dessert (P)	419th NFS	1		1st Lt. Robert P. Lutz (P)	414th NFS	1	
2nd Lt. Lane K. Thompson (R/O)				2nd Lt. Wallace A. Morrissette (R/O)			
S/Sgt. Frank A. McCormack (G)				1st Lt. Edgar E. Merriman (P)	422nd NFS	1	
2nd Lt. George M. Ellings (P)	418th NFS	1		2nd Lt. Delbert W. Dow (R/O)			
F/O Milton Burman (R/O)				1st Lt. Harold E. Michels (P)	419th NFS	1	
2nd Lt. Robert L. Ferguson (P)	6th NFS	1		F/O Verna J. Morgan (R/O)			
2nd Lt. Charles A. Ward (R/O)				Sgt. Joseph C. Snyder (G)			
Sgt. Leroy F. Miozzi (G)				1st Lt. Roy E. Oaskes (P)	547th NFS	1	
F/O Donald U. Gendreau (P)	549th NFS	1		1st Lt. Ralph N. Jacomin (R/O)			
F/O Elia A. Chiappinelli (R/O)				S/Sgt. Ralph M. Knight (G)			
S/Sgt. William S. Dare (G)				2nd Lt. David J. Pahlka (P)	421st NFS	1	
2nd Lt. Orin K. Goodrich (P)	414th NFS	1		2nd Lt. Ralph V. Hulsey (R/O)			
2nd Lt. Raymond J. Lane (R/O)				T/Sgt. Harold L. Cobb (G)			
1st Lt. Richard R. Gray (P)	425th NFS	1		2nd Lt. Robert C. Pew (P)	421st NFS	1	
1st Lt. Jack W. Robinson (R/O)			(2 total)	2nd Lt. John B. Cutshall (R/O)			
1st Lt. Thomas J. Greenfield (P)	414th NFS	1		S/Sgt. Ralph H. McDaniel (G)			
2nd Lt. Joseph E. Swartz (R/O)				2nd Lt. Carl R. Remington (P)	421st NFS	1	
2nd Lt. Curtis R. Griffitts, Jr. (P)	418th NFS	1		F/O William E. Boze (R/O)			
2nd Lt. Myron G. Bigler (R/O)				T/Sgt. Brady W. Swinney (G)			
2nd Lt. Jerome M. Hanson (P)	6th NFS	1		1st Lt. Malcolm L. Ritchie (P)	418th NFS	1	
2nd Lt. William K. Wallace (R/O)				F/O Vincent Wertin (R/O)			(4 total)
1st Lt. Harry W. Heise (P)	426th NFS	1		2nd Lt. Raymond L. Romens (P)	422nd NFS	1	
F/O Robert C. Brock (R/O)							

Confirmed Aircrew Victories

Aircrew	Squadron	Total kills	Notes	Aircrew	Squadron	Total kills	Notes
2nd Lt. Joseph R. Morin (R/O)				F/O Alfred H. Borges, Jr. (R/O)			
1st Lt. William F. Ross (P)	418th NFS	1		1st Lt. James L. Thompson (P)	425th NFS	1	
2nd Lt. Raymond L. Duethman (R/O)				F/O Joseph E. Downey (R/O)			
1st Lt. Kenneth R. Schrieber (P)	547th NFS	1		1st Lt. Harold B. Whittern (P)	418th NFS	1	
2nd Lt. Bonnie B. Rucks (R/O)			(3 total)	2nd Lt. Bunyan A. Crain, Jr. (R/O)			
2nd Lt. James F. Schroth (P)	419th NFS	1		Capt. John J. Wilfong (P)	426th NFS	1	
F/O Fred R. James (R/O)				2nd Lt. Glenn E. Ashley (R/O)			
S/Sgt. Glen O. Deforrest (G)				1st Lt. Garth E. Peterson (P)	425th NFS	0	2 V-1s
1st Lt. Thomas W. Schultz (P)	548th NFS	1		2nd Lt. John A. Howe (R/O)			
F/O Ployer P. Hill (R/O)							
S/Sgt. Benjamin J. Boscardin (G)			(2 total)				
Capt. Robert R. Scott (P)	426th NFS	1					
F/O Charles W. Phillips (R/O)							
1st Lt. Arthur C. Shepherd (P)	548th NFS	1					
1st Lt. Arvid L. Shulenberger (R/O)							
M/Sgt. Donald E. Meech (G)							
1st Lt. Hoke Smith (P)	421st NFS	1					
2nd Lt. Robert H. Bremer (R/O)							
Sgt. James W. Pilling (G)							
1st Lt. Walter Stacey (P)	425th NFS	1					
2nd Lt. Stephen F. Mason (R/O)							
F/O John J. Szpila (P)	6th NFS	1					

*The Office of Air Force History records show Captain Annis with full credit. 547th NFS records and those of the Champlin Fighter Museum give him half credit, and 1st Lt. Roy E. Oakes, who was flying a 547th NFS P-38 with the P-61, received half credit for his joint actions in this combat.

Abbreviations:
E/A enemy aircraft
G gunner
P pilot
R/O radio observer

Notes:

1. Listing is presented in descending order of total aerial victories accredited for each pilot, and secondarily in alphabetical order by pilots' last name, if more than one pilot had the same number of enemy aircraft destroyed.

2. If crew members other than pilot did not participate in all of the kills, the number of kills that he did accumulate will show in the Notes column.

3. If crew members other than pilot have a total number of kills different from the pilot (that is, credit for E/A destroyed while flying with another pilot), the number that he did will be annotated in the Notes column in parentheses [e.g. (4 total)].

Appendix C

Black Widow Aces

The *United States Air Force Dictionary* defines "ace" as follows: "ace, n. An expert combat pilot; specif., one credited with not less than five victories." It defines "victory" as: "victory, n. 1. The overcoming of an enemy in battle; an instance of this. 2. Specif. An instance in which an airman destroys an enemy aircraft in air-to-air combat, as in 'he had 10 victories and 2 probables.'"

There were some 800 members of the US Army Air Forces in World War II who acquired this distinction. For the approximately fifteen months that the Black Widow flew in combat, it produced its share of aces.

The sources listed in Appendix B were used to gather the following data on airmen who were accredited with five or more enemy aircraft destroyed. As with much of life, all is not black and white. Can only a pilot be an ace? Or is the radar operator so entitled if he participates in the destruction of five or more enemy aircraft? Do only manned aircraft count, or do the German V-1s in the European theater also count toward this coveted title?

In an attempt to answer these questions, I turned to two sources: *Five Down and Glory* by Gene Gurney, and *American Aces of World War II and Korea* by William N. Hess.

Hess states (page 16) that V-1s were counted, and he includes them in his confirmed victory list for Ninth Air Force aces. Hess does not include them in the pilot's totals, however, and lists them in the Remarks column of his listings. There is also a difference of opinion between these gentlemen concerning kill credit to the R/O. Gurney gives credit to both pilot and R/O, and his listing comingles and lists them in alphabetical order. On the other hand, Hess lists the R/O below the pilot he flew with.

These accreditation deviations make a difference in determining the number of aces associated with the P-61. In the case of giv-

ing equal weight to V-1s, the 422nd NFS's team of Lt. Robert O. Elmore (pilot) and Lt. Leonard F. Mapes (R/O), who were credited with four manned enemy aircraft and one V-1, would be accorded the title ace. Likewise would Lt. Robert F. Graham, also of the 422nd NFS, who as an R/O participated in the destruction of five enemy aircraft, but with two different pilots.

Following are the airmen and their accredited kills:

Lt. Herman E. Ernst (P)
Lt. Edward H. Kopsel (R/O)
422nd NFS
Confirmed victories

July 16, 1944	V-1
Nov. 27, 1944	Me 110
Dec. 17, 1944	Ju 87
Dec. 27, 1944	Ju 188
Mar. 2, 1945	Ju 87
Mar. 2, 1945	Ju 87

Damaged

Dec. 27, 1944	Ju 88
Mar. 2, 1945	Me 110

Lt. Paul A. Smith (P)
Lt. Robert E. Tierney (R/O)
422nd NFS
Confirmed victories

Oct. 4, 1944	Me 410
Nov. 27, 1944	V-1
Nov. 27, 1944	He 111
Dec. 25, 1944	Ju 88
Dec. 26, 1944	Ju 188
Dec. 26, 1944	Ju 188

Probable victory

Aug. 7, 1944	Me 110

Maj. Carroll C. Smith (P)
Lt. Philip B. Porter (R/O)
418th NFS
Confirmed victories

Oct. 7, 1944	Dinah Mk. II
Dec. 29, 1944	Irving
Dec. 29, 1944	Irving
Dec. 30, 1944	Rufe
Dec. 30, 1944	Frank

Major Smith is also credited with two additional confirmed and two probable victories while flying P-38s in searchlight cooperative missions. This makes Smith the leading night fighter pilot in the Army Air Forces.

Lt. Eugene D. Axtell (P)
422nd NFS
Confirmed victories

Dec. 27, 1944	Ju 88[1]
Dec. 27, 1944	Ju 188[1]
Jan. 1, 1945	Ju 188[2]
Apr. 11, 1945	Ju 52[3]
Apr. 11, 1945	Ju 52[3]

Probable victories

Aug. 6, 1944	Do 217[4]
Aug. 25, 1944	Ju 188[4]

[1]Lt. Bernard Orzel, R/O, also participated.
[2]Lt. John U. Morris, Jr., R/O, also participated.
[3]Lt. Creel H. Morrison, R/O, also participated.
[4]Lt. Joseph F. Crew, R/O, also participated.

Lt. Robert F. Graham (R/O)
422nd NFS
Confirmed victories

Nov. 26, 1944	He 111[1]
Dec. 17, 1944	Fw 190[1]
Dec. 17, 1944	Me 110[1]
Dec. 17, 1944	He 111[1]
Mar. 21, 1945	Do 217[2]

Probable victory

Dec. 17, 1944	He 111[1]

[1]Lt. Robert G. Bolinder, pilot, also participated
[2]Capt. Raymond A. Anderson, pilot, also participated.

Lt. Robert O. Elmore (P)
Lt. Leonard F. Mapes (R/O)
422nd NFS
Confirmed victories

July 17, 1944	V-1
Dec. 17, 1944	Ju 88
Dec. 22, 1944	He 111
Apr. 11, 1945	Ju 52
Apr. 11, 1945	Ju 52

Appendix D

P–61 Serial Numbers

P-61 Serial Numbers

Air Force Serial numbers	C/N range	Designation	Qty.[1]	FAA "N" Nos.	Redesignations	Air Force Serial numbers	C/N range	Designation	Qty.[1]	FAA "N" Nos.	Redesignations
41-19509/19510	701/702	XP-61-NO	2								
	703	Static test	1			42-39461/39462	980/981	P-61B-2-NO			
41-18876/18887	704/715	YP-61-NO	13			42-39463/39465	982/984	P-61B-1-NO			
41-18888	716	YP-61-NO		N60358		42-39466	985	P-61B-2-NO			
42-5485/5529	717/761	P-61A-1-NO	45			42-39467/39470	986/989	P-61B-1-NO			
42-5530/5558	762/790	P-61A-5-NO	35			42-39471/39473	990/992	P-61B-2-NO			
42-5559	791	P-61A-5-NO			XP-61C/XP-61D	42-39474	993	P-61B-1-NO			
42-5560/5564	792/796	P-61A-5-NO				42-39475	994	P-61B-2-NO			
42-5565/5586	797/818	P-61A-10-NO	100			42-39476/39477	995/996	P-61B-1-NO			
42-5587	819	P-61A-10-NO			XP-61C/XP-61D	42-39478/39480	997/999	P-61B-2-NO			
42-5588/5604	820/836	P-61A-10-NO				42-39481/39482	1000/1001	P-61B-1-NO			
42-5605/5606	837/838	P-61A-11-NO	20			42-39483/39490	1002/1009	P-61B-2-NO			
42-5607	839	P-61A-10-NO				42-39491	1010	P-61B-1-NO			
42-5608/5614	840/846	P-61A-11-NO				42-39492/39493	1011/1012	P-61B-2-NO			
42-5615/5634	847/866	P-61A-10-NO				42-39494	1013	P-61B-1-NO			
42-39348/39374	867/893	P-61A-10-NO				42-39495	1014	P-61B-2-NO			
42-39375/39384	894/903	P-61A-11-NO				42-39496/39497	1015/1016	P-61B-1-NO			
42-39387	906	P-61A-11-NO				42-39498	1017	P-61B-5-NO	3		XP-61B
42-39388/39397	907/916	P-61A-10-NO				42-39499/39500	1018/1019	P-61B-5-NO			
42-39398/39401	917/920	P-61B-1-NO	62			42-39501/39547	1020/1066	P-61B-6-NO	47		
42-39402	921	P-61B-2-NO	38			42-39548	1067	P-61B-10-NO	45		
42-39403/39405	922/924	P-61B-1-NO				42-39549	1068	P-61B-10-NO			XP-61E/XF-15
42-39406	925	P-61B-2-NO				42-39550/39556	1069/1075	P-61B-10-NO			
42-39407	926	P-61B-1-NO				42139557	1076	P-61B-10-NO			XP-61E
42-39408	927	P-61B-2-NO				42-39558/39572	1077/1091	P-61B-10-NO			
42-39409/39411	928/930	P-61B-1-NO				42-39573/39611	1092/1130	P-61B-15-NO	153		
42-39412/39414	931/933	P-61B-2-NO				42-39612	1131	P-61B-10-NO			
42-39415/39417	934/936	P-61B-1-NO				42-39613	1132	P-61B-25-NO	7		
42-39418	937	P-61B-2-NO				42-39614	1133	P-61B-15-NO			
42-39419[6]	938	P-61B-1-NO		NX30020/ N30020		42-39615	1134	P-61B-10-NO			
						42-39616	1135	P-61B-15-NO			
42-39420/39423	939/942	P-61B-1-NO				42-39617	1136	P-61B-10-NO			
42-39424	943	P-61B-2-NO				42-39618	1137	P-61B-15-NO			
42-39425	944	P-61B-1-NO				42-39619	1138	P-61B-10-NO			
42-39426	945	P-61B-2-NO				42-39620	1139	P-61B-16-NO	6		
42-39427	946	P-61B-1-NO				42-39621[2]	1140	P-61B-11-NO	5		F2T-1
42-39428	947	P-61B-2-NO				42-39622	1141	P-61B-16-NO			
42-39429	948	P-61B-1-NO				42-39623	1142	P-61B-11-NO			
42-39430	949	P-61B-2-NO				42-39624	1143	P-61B-16-NO			
42-39431	950	P-61B-1-NO				42-39625	1144	P-61B-11-NO			
42-39432	951	P-61B-2-NO				42-39626	1145	P-61B-16-NO			
42-39433/39451	952/970	P-61B-1-NO				42-39627	1146	P-61B-11-NO			
42-39452/39456	971/975	P-61B-2-NO				42-39628	1147	P-61B-16-NO			
42-39457/39460	976/979	P-61B-1-NO				42-39629	1148	P-61B-11-NO			

Air Force Serial numbers	C/N range	Designation	Qty.[1]	FAA "N" Nos.	Redesignations
42-39630	1149	P-61B-16-NO			
42-39631/39633	1150/1152	P-61B-15-NO			
42-39634	1153	P-61B-10-NO			
42-39635[2]	1154	P-61B-10-NO			F2T-1
42-39636	1155	P-61B-10-NO			
42-39637/39639	1156/1158	P-61B-15-NO			
42-39640/39641	1159/1160	P-61B-10-NO			
42-39642	1161	P-61B-15-NO			
42-39643	1162	P-61B-10-NO			
42-39644	1163	P-61B-15-NO			
42-39645	1164	P-61B-10-NO			
42-39646	1165	P-61B-15-NO			
42-39647	1166	P-61B-10-NO			
42-39648	1167	P-61B-15-NO			
42-39649[2]	1168	P-61B-15-NO			F2T-1
42-39650	1169	P-61B-10-NO			
42-39651[2]	1170	P-61B-15-NO			F2T-1
42-39652	1171	P-61B-10-NO			
42-39653[2]	1172	P-61B-15-NO			F2T-1
42-39654	1173	P-61B-10-NO			
42-39655[2]	1174	P-61B-15-NO			F2T-1
42-39656	1175	P-61B-10-NO			
42-39657	1176	P-61B-15-NO			
42-39658	1177	P-61B-10-NO			
42-39659/39661	1178/1180	P-61B-15-NO			
42-39662	1181	P-61B-10-NO			
42-39663/39665	1182/1184	P-61B-15-NO			
42-39666/39667	1185/1186	P-61B-10-NO			
42-39668	1187	P-61B-15-NO			
42-39669[2]	1188	P-61B-15-NO			F2T-1
42-39670/39726	1189/1245	P-61B-15-NO			
42-39727[2]	1246	P-61B-15-NO			F2T-1
42-39728/39757	1247/1276	P-61B-15-NO			
43-8231/8236	1277/1282	P-61B-25-NO			
43-8237/8265	1283/1311	P-61B-20-NO	84		
43-8266[2]	1312	P-61B-20-NO			F2T-1
43-8267/8273	1313/1319	P-61B-20-NO			
43-8274[2]	1320	P-61B-20-NO			F2T-1
43-8275/8306	1321/1352	P-61B-20-NO			
43-8307[2]	1353	P-61B-20-NO			F2T-1
43-8308[2]	1354	P-61B-20-NO			F2T-1
43-8309/8320	1355/1366	P-61B-20-NO			
43-8321/8329	1367/1375	P-61C-1-NO	41		
43-8330[3]	1376	P-61C-1-NO			
43-8331/8334	1377/1380	P-61C-1-NO			
43-8335	1381	P-61C-1-NO			XF-15A
43-8336/8337	1382/1383	P-61C-1-NO			
43-8338	1384	P-61C-1-NO			XP-61F[4]
43-8339/8348	1385/1394	P-61C-1-NO			
43-8349	1395	P-61C-1-NO		N4905V[5]	

Air Force Serial numbers	C/N range	Designation	Qty.[1]	FAA "N" Nos.	Redesignations
43-8350/8356	1396/1402	P-61C-1-NO			
43-8357	1403	P-61C-1-NO		N5094V	
43-8358/8361	1404/1407	P-61C-1-NO			
43-8362/8437	1408/1483	P-61C		Canceled	
45-001/400	1484/1883	P-61C		Canceled	
45-59300[5][6][7]	3201	F-15A-1-NO	20	N5093V/ N9768Z	RF-61C
45-59301/59319	3202/3220	F-15A-1-NO			RF-61C
45-59320/59335	3221/3236	F-15A-5-NO	16		RF-61C
45-59336/59474	3237/3375	F-15A		Canceled	

Notes:

[1]Quantity per block will be given at the initial listing of each block number.

[2]These aircraft were transferred to the Department of the Navy. The authors have not been able to correlate AF serial number to Navy BuNo at this time. For BuNos, see separate BuNo listing.

[3]These are not the only P-61/F-15 aircraft used by the NACA, but they seem to be the only ones assigned NACA serial numbers. 43-8330, NACA330 and 45-59300, NACA 111.

[4]This project never got beyond the proposal stage. The aircraft was never modified.

[5]The FAA has this aircraft listed incorrectly as serial number 43-8364.

[6]USF Number: 42-39419, E53 and 45-59300, E35.

[7]Foreign Registry, Mexico XB-FUJ.

Comments:

With the change in the USAF's aircraft designation system in June, 1948, all P-61s became F-61s and F-15As became RF-61Cs. It has not been determined yet (by the authors) whether or not the RF-61C's retained the block numbers assigned to the F-15As. It is of interest to note that in the model designation changeover some of the F-15A's were erroneously changed to RF-61As rather than Cs on the USAF's individual Aircraft Record Cards.

As the F-61s were phased out of operational use, many were redesignated with a "T" prefix (TF-61) to indicate that they were being relegated to training duties only. Others were loaned to government agencies other than the Air Force or to civilian agencies. Aircraft in this classification had an "E" prefix (EF-61). A few P-61As that remained in service after the war and some early Bs were classified as obsolete and had a "Z" prefix (ZF-61). By June 1950 all F-61s had been phased out of operational squadrons. In 1952 all RF/F-61s were declared surplus by the Air Force.

As with most aircraft after the war, the '61s had "Buzz Letters" assigned.

P-61	"PK"	F-15A	"FH"
F-61	"FK"	RF-61C	"FH"

F2T-1 BUNOs:

52750 through 52761

Appendix E

P–61 Specifications

Model	Engine ratings (bhp/alt) takeoff war emergency military normal	Prop	Speed (mph) max/hp/alt landing (at designed wt.)	Climb (minutes) time-to-altitude service ceiling (at designed wt.)	Takeoff & landing (over 50 ft. obstacle) takeoff landing (at designed wt.)	Spec. Range (miles/mph/alt) ferry normal design
XP-61 (R-2800-10)	2,000 2,000/1,000[2] 1,650/22,500 1,675/5,500 1,500/21,500	Curtiss 12-2 F.F. Const. Spd.	370/3,090/20,900 95	9/20,000 33,100	1,575 2,150	1,465/200/10,000 1,465/200/10,000 1,200/200/10,000
YP-61 (R-2800-10)	Same	Same	Same 93	Same	Same	1,450/200/10,000 1,450/200/10,000 1,200/200/10,000
P-61A-1 (R-2800-10)	Same	Same	(at 27,600 lb.) 360/-/25,000 93	(at 27,600 lb.) 10.1/20,000 33,100	(at 28,000 lb. TO) 2,300 1,700	1,100/227/10,000 460/323/25,000 410/310/10,000
P-61A-5, 10, 11 R-2800-65	2,000 2,040/12,800[3] 1,930/17,000 2,000/1,000 1,650/22,500 1,675/5,500 1,550/21,500	Same	(at 28,000 lb.) 369/-/20,000 93	(at 28,000 lb.) 10.3/20,000 33,100	Same	2,225/221/10,000 400/318/25,000 375/322/10,000
P-61B-1, 2, 5, 6, 10, 11 (R-2800-65)	Same	Same	Same	Same	Same	3,000/200/15,000 400/318/25,000 375/322/10,000
P-61B-15, 16, 20, 25 (R-2800-65)	Same	Same	(at 29,700 lb.) 366/-/20,000 93	(at 29,700 lb.) 12/12,000 33,100	Same	Same
P-61C-1 (R-2800-73)	2,100 2,800/32,500 2,100/30,000 1,700/30,000	Curtiss 12-8 F.F. Const. Spd.	430/-/30,000 87	14.6/30,000 41,000	2,000 1,700	1,725/190/50,000 415/314/25,000 330/307/10,000
XP-61D (R-2800-77)	2,100 2,800/30,000 2,100/30,000 1,700/30,000	Same	430/5,600/30,000 90	13.5/30,000 43,000	2,000 1,600	3,000/205/- -/-/- 1,050/197/-
XP-61E (R-2800-65)	2,000 2,040/12,800[3] 1,930/17,000 2,000/1,000 1,650/22,500 1,675/5,500 1,550/21,500	Curtiss 12-2 F.F. Const. Spd.	376/3,860/17,000	13/20,000 30,000	2,700 1,500	3,750/-/- -/-/- 2,250/-/-

[1]Source:
  Army Aircraft Characteristics, Report Number TSEST-A2, dated Mar. 16, 1946; Monthly Chart, Armament and Bomb Installations, dated Sept. 1, 1945.
[2]War emergency ratings quoted directly from manufacturer's specifications.
[3]War emergency ratings with Ram quoted directly from Tech.

P-61 Specifications

Model	Span	Length	Height	Tread	Wing area	Empty weight	Design gross wt.	Fuel
XP-61	66′	48′ 11.2″	14′ 8.2″	17′ 1″	663.3 sq-ft	21,695 lb.	27,575 lb.	640 gal. 640 540
YP-61	Same	Same	Same	Same	Same	21,910	27,950	640 640 540
P-61A (all blocks)	Same	Same	Same	17′ 2″	664	20,965	27,000	640[1] 640 550
P-61B-1, 2, 5, 6, 10, 11	Same	49′ 7.2″	Same	Same	Same	21,215	27,350	640[2] 640 550
P-61B-15, 16, 20, 25	Same	Same	Same	Same	Same	22,000	27,800	640[3] 640 550
P-61C-1	Same	Same	Same	Same	Same	24,000	31,105	640[3] 640 528
XP-61D	Same	48′ 11.2″	Same	Same	Same	23,205	29,208	640[3] 640 528
XP-61E	Same	49′ 7.2″	13′ 5″	Same	662	21,350	31,425	2,398[3] 1,158 1,158

Notes:

[1] P-61A-11 was equipped with two wing racks capable of carrying up to one 310 gallon external fuel tank each, bringing maximum fuel to 1,260 gallons.

[2] P-61B-2, 6 and 11 were equipped with two wing racks capable of carrying up to one 310 gallon external fuel tank each, and the P-61B-10 was equipped with four wing racks. Maximum fuel for P-61B-2, 6 and 11 was 1,260 gallons, and for the P-61B-10, 1,880 gallons.

[3] Capable of carrying four external 310 gallon fuel tanks on wing racks totaling 1,880 gallons, except for the P-61B-16 which reverted back to two wing racks.

Appendix F

Sources

Military drawings

S45K572, General Arrangement Dod, P-61 Long Range Escort Fighter, 23 August 1944

Northrop Aircraft, Inc. documentation

Report No. D-2, Basic Dimension Report, Model and Description, Night Interceptor Pursuit XP-61, YP-61, P-61A, B

Report No. NS-6, Zap Wing Conversion of OS2U-1

Report No. NS-8A, Model Specification, Night Interceptor Pursuit Air Corps Model XP-61

Report No. NS-8C, Model Specification, Night Interceptor Pursuit Air Corps Model P-61

Report No. NS-8D, Model Specification, Night Interceptor Pursuit Army Air Force Model P-61B

Report No. NS-8E, Model Specification, Night Interceptor Pursuit Army Air Force Model P-61C

Report No. NS-8F, Model Specification, Night Interceptor Pursuit Army Air Force Model XP-61D

Report No. NS-17, Model Specification, Long Range Escort Fighter Army Air Force Model XP-61E

Report No. NS-20, Model Specification, Long Range Photo Reconnaissance Army Air Force Model XF-15

Report No. NS-20, Revision 1, Model Specification, Long Range Photo Reconnaissance Army Air Force XF-15A

Report No. NS-20A, Model Specification, Long Range Photo Reconnaissance Army Air Force F-15A-1

  Note: Supplement No. 1 added F-15A-5, serial number 45-59335

Drawing No. 502948 General Arrangement (Three View), Project VNT

Drawing No. 504944 General Arrangement (Three View), Model XP-61

Drawing No. 505100 General Arrangement (Three View), Models XP-61, YP-61, P-61A-1, P-61B-1

Drawing No. 530338, General Arrangement (Three View), Model XP-61E

Northrop Aircraft, Inc. NEWS releases:

  "History of the Black Widow" (late 1945)

  "New Photo Plane Proves Versatility of Northrop Design"—*The Northrop Reporter* (early 1946)

  "The Northrop Retractable Aileron System" (May 1946)

  "Newest Black Widow Is Nation's First Peacetime Warplane" (Sept. 3, 1945)

  Stephens, Moye, Chief Production Test Pilot, *Operation of the "Retractable Aileron" System of the Black Widow P-61 Night Fighter,* Northrop Aircraft, Inc., Sept. 15, 1944

Military publications

Aircraft History Card (NAVAER-1925(9-44))

Airplane Characteristics and Performance (monthly and quarterly charts), Air Materiel Command, Engineering Division, Technical Data Laboratory

Armament and Bomb Installations (monthly and quarterly charts), Air Materiel Command, Engineering Division, Technical Data Laboratory

Individual Aircraft Record Card

Pilot Training Manual For the Black Widow

Report of Serial Numbers Assigned to Aircraft on Active Air Force Contracts (AFPI Form 41)

Standard Aircraft Characteristics, P-61C Black Widow

Tactical Planning Characteristics & Performance Chart (P-61)

TO 00-20A-2-P-61, U.S. Army Air Forces Aircraft Inspection and Maintenance Guide for P-61 Series Aircraft

TO 01-15FB-1, Pilot's Flight Operating Instructions For Army Model P-61A Airplane

AN 01-15FB-1, Pilot's Flight Operating Instructions For Army Models P-61A and P-61B Airplanes

TO 01-15FB-2, P-61A Service Instructions

AN 01-15FB-4, Parts Catalog For P-61A and P-61B Airplanes

AN 01-15FC-1, Handbook-Flight Operating Instructions, USAF Series F-61C Aircraft

AN 01-15FC-2, Erection and Maintenance Instructions For Model P-61C Airplane

AN 01-15FC-4, Parts Catalog For F-61C Airplanes

AN 01-15JA-1, Handbook-Flight Operating Instructions, USAF Series RF-61C Aircraft

AN 01-15JA-2, Erection and Maintenance Instructions For Army Model F-15A Airplane

AN 01-15JA-4, Parts Catalog For Model F-15A Airplane

AN 11-70A-26, Operation and Service Instructions For Remote Control Turret Systems Models 2CFR12C2 and 2CFR12C3

Military reports

Accelerated Service Test of P-61C Type Aircraft Nos. 43-8325, 43-8322 and 43-8337, Memorandum Report TSFTE-2068, 14 April 1947, Prepared by Albert L. Jackson, Jr.

Acceptance Performance Tests-XP-61 Airplane, Army Air Forces Serial Number 41-19509, Memorandum Report ENG-19-1605-A

Aircraft Model Designation, Report No. TSEST-A7, 1 June 1946

Cold Weather Test of P-61A Type Aircraft, Army Air Forces Board Project (M-1)16b, 20 June 1944, Prepared by Capt. F. E. Graizer, A.C.

Escape From High Speed Aircraft, Memorandum Report TSEAC11-45341-1-2, 9 August 1946, Prepared by Lt. Col. F. S. Cofer, Jr., A.C., Lt. Col. H. M. Sweeney, A.C., and Carl E. Frenier

Final report of the Procurement, Inspection, Testing and Acceptance of Northrop Airplane Model XP-61, Army Air Forces Technical Report No. 5070, Prepared by Capt. W. G. Logen, A.C.

Final Report of the Development, Procurement, Performance, and Acceptance of the XP-61D Airplane, AFTR 5693, 27 April 1948

Final Report on the Test of YP-61 Airplanes, Army Air Forces Proving Ground Command Project (M-5)17, 9 June 1944, Prepared by 2nd Lt. John L. Decker, A.C.

Human Subject Ejection Test from P-61B Airplane, Memorandum Report TSEAC11-45341-2-1, 26 August 1946, Prepared by H. W. Fouch

Operational Suitability of the YP-61 Airplane, Army Air Forces Board Project (M-1)16, 20 June 1944, Prepared by Maj. B. R. Muldoon, A.C.

Performance Flight Tests of the Northrop Black Widow P-61A Airplane, AAF No. 42-5488, Memorandum Report ENG-47-1796-A, 28 August 1944, Prepared by Willard A. Burrell and Capt. Jack D. Onerem, A.C.

689 Engineering Acceptance Inspection of the Northrop Aircraft Incorporated, F-15A Airplane, AAF Serial No. 45-59000, Memorandum Report TSEAC8-4092-8-9, 10 July 1946, Prepared by A. L. Corriveau and J. L. Carrell

Miscellaneous data

Records of the Army Air Forces (P-61), 1941-1945, National Archives Record Group No. 18.

Beavers, William W. *The Northrop P-61 "Black Widow"–America's First Night Fighter*, Fresno State College, History 199, Jan. 12, 1965.

The P-61 Gunfire-Control System, Report GET-1144, General Electric Company, Aircraft Armament School, Nov. 4, 1942.

Hall, L. R., Capt. *Notes on Nightfighting*, Army Air Forces School of Applied Tactics, 1943.

Factual Aircraft Accident Report-General Accident, P-61B Accident of 23 August 1963.

Radio Transcript, *Top of the Evening*, with Ted Malone, Dec. 19-20, 1944.

National Advisory Committee for Aeronautics reports

Ashkenas, I. L. *The Development of a Lateral Control System for Use with Large-Span Flaps*, Technical Note 1015, Northrop Aircraft, Inc., January 1946.

Nissen, James M. et al. *Correlation of the Drag Characteristics of a P-51B Airplane Obtained from High-Speed Wind-Tunnel and Flight Test*, Advance Confidential Report 4K02, Ames Aeronautical Laboratory, Moffett Field, Calif., February 1945.

Skoog, Richard B. *A Comparison of Two Flight-Test Procedures For The Determination of Aileron Control Capabilities of an Airplane*, Advance Restricted Report 5E22, Ames Aeronautical Laboratory, Moffett Field, Calif., July 1945.

Spahr, J. Richard. *Lateral-Control Characteristics of Various Spoiler Arrangements as Measured in Flight*, Technical Note No. 1123, Ames Aeronautical Laboratory, Moffett Field, Calif., January 1947.

Spahr, J. Richard and Don R. Christophersen. *Lateral-Control Characteristics of an Airplane Equipped with Full-Span Zap Flaps and Simple Circular-Arc-Type Ailerons*, Memorandum Report September 1944, Ames Aeronautical Laboratory, Moffett Field, Calif., September 1944.

Spahr, J. Richard and Don R. Christophersen. *Measurements in Flight of the Stability, Lateral-Control, and Stalling Characteristics of an Airplane Equipped with Full-Span Zap Flaps and Spoiler-Type Ailerons*, Memorandum Report December 1943, Ames Aeronautical Laboratory, Moffett Field, Calif., December 1943.

Tolefson, Harold B. *Preliminary Analysis of NACA Measurements of Atmospheric Turbulence Within a Thunderstorm–U.S. Weather Bureau Thunderstorm Project*, Technical Note 1233, Langley Memorial Aeronautical Laboratory, Langley Field, Va., March 1947.

Books

Anderson, Fred. *Northrop: An Aeronautical History*. Century City, Calif.: Northrop, 1976.

Belote, James H. and William M. Belote. *Typhoon of Steel: The Battle for Okinawa*. New York: Harper & Row, 1970.

Birdsall, Steve. *Flying Buccaneers*. Garden City, N.Y.: Doubleday, 1977.

Brown, K. S. et al., comp. *United States Army and Air Force Fighters 1916–1961*. Ed. Bruce Robertson. Letchworth, England: Harleyford, 1961.

Coleman, Ted. *Jack Northrop and the Flying Wing*. New York: Paragon, 1988.

Copp, DeWitt S. *Forged in Fire*. Garden City, N.Y.: Doubleday, 1982.

Cornelius, Wanda and Thayne Short. *Ding Hao: America's Air War in China, 1937–1945*. Gretna, La.: Pelican, 1980.

Craven, Wesley Frank and James Lea Cate, eds. *The Army Air Forces In World War II*. 7 vols. Chicago: Univ. of Chicago P., 1948.

Gurney, Gene, Capt. USAF. *Five Down and Glory*. Ed. Mark P. Friedlander, Jr. New York: Putnam, 1958.

Hess, William N. *Pacific Sweep*. Garden City, N.Y.: Doubleday, 1974
——. *The American Aces of World War II and Korea*. New York: Arco, 1968

Maurer, Maurer, ed. *Air Force Combat Units of World War II*. New York: Franklin Watts, 1963.
——. *Combat Squadrons of the Air Force*. Washington: US Government Printing Office, 1969.

Morrison, Wilbur H. *Point of No Return*. Times, 1979.

Rust, Kenn C. *Fifteenth Air Force Story*. Temple City, Calif.: Historical Aviation Album, 1976.
——. *Fifth Air Force Story*. Temple City, Calif.: Historical Aviation Album, 1973.
——. *Fourteenth Air Force Story*. Temple City, Calif.: Historical Aviation Album, 1977.
——. *Seventh Air Force Story*. Temple City, Calif.: Historical Aviation Album, 1979.
——. *The 9th Air Force in World War II*. Fall Brook, Calif.: Aero, 1967.
——. *Twelfth Air Force Story*. Temple City, Calif.: Historical Aviation Album, 1975.

Sargent, Frederic O., comp. *Night Fighters: An Unofficial History of the 415th Night Fighter Squadron*. Madison, Wis.: Sargent, 1946.

Periodical articles

"All in a Night's Work." *Air Force*, December 1944.

"Design Details of the Northrop P-61, Part I." *Aero Digest*, Nov. 1, 1945.

"Design Details of the Northrop P-61, Part II." *Aero Digest*, Dec. 1, 1945.

"How to Fly a P-61." *Air News with Air Tech*, September 1945.

"P-61." *Air News with Air Tech*, September 1945.

Boesen, Victor. "The Legal Eagle." *Skyway*, October 1946.

Buchanan, R. E., Lt. "P-61s on the Prowl." *Flying Age*, July 1945.

Harald, Eric. "P-61 Black Widow." *Skyways*, September 1944.

Harper, Harmon H., 1st Lt. "Wings Against the Storm." *AAF Review*, August 1946.

Holt, William K., Lt., USMC. "Fly By Night." *Skyways*, September 1945.

Kratz, Winston W., Lt. Col. "Night Fighters-Commandos of the Air." *Air Force*, January 1944.

Leford, Dale, Maj. "The Last Kill." *Air Classics*, May-June 1965 (error by magazine; his first name is Bruce).

Littrell, Gaither. "The 'Black Widow' Boys." *Flying*, June 1945.

Munson, Donn H. "Nipponese Nightmare." *Yank*, 1944.

Myers, John. "Scourge of the Night Skies." *Flying Aces*, March 1945.

Silsbee, Nathaniel F. and Ralph W. Brown. "The Air Force Flies the Weather." *Aero Digest,* April 1948.

Smith, Carroll C. "My Sweetheart Is a Black Widow." *Popular Science,* July 1945.

Smith, David. "Black Widows in Britain." *Aviation News,* Dec. 30, 1983–Jan. 12, 1984.

Stephens, Moye. "The Black Widow's Retractable Ailerons." *Western Flying,* December, 1944.

Winters, M. M. "Evolution of the P-61 Black Widow." *Skyways,* September 1945.

Wright, Jay E. "The First and Last F-15A." *American Aviation, Historical Society,* fall 1969.